WHO TELLETH A TALE OF UNSPEAKING DEATH?

DUBLIN DEATH STUDIES 2

WHO TELLETH A TALE OF UNSPEAKING DEATH?

DUBLIN DEATH STUDIES 2

Edited by

Wolfgang Marx

Carysfort Press

A Carysfort Press Book in association with Peter Lang
Who telleth a tale of unspeaking death? Dublin Death Studies 2
Edited by Wolfgang Marx

First published in Ireland in 2017 as a paperback original by
Carysfort Press, 58 Woodfield, Scholarstown Road
Dublin 16, Ireland

ISBN 978-1-78997-032-6
©2017 Copyright remains with the authors

Typeset by Joseph Brady

Cover design by Joseph Brady and Alun Carr

Caution: All rights reserved. No part of this book may be printed or reproduced or utilized in any form or by any electronic, mechanical, or other means, now known or hereafter invented including photocopying and recording, or in any information storage or retrieval system without permission in writing from the publishers.

Contents

Acknowledgements   vii

Introduction   1
    Wolfgang Marx

1 | Illustrious Corpses: Burying Irish Nationalist Heroes   7
    Michael Laffan

2 | Crying by Singing Out: Performing the Cry-die of North West Cameroon in Dublin   31
    Sheryl Lynch

3 | The Tomb of Pietro da Cortona in Santi Luca e Martina al Foro   49
    Corinna Ricasoli

4 | How Tocqueville became 'Tocqueville' – Gustave de Beaumont's Letters from Cannes and the First Edition of *Memoir, Letters, and Remains of Alexis de Tocqueville*   75
    Andreas Hess

5 | Philosophical Reflections on Reality and Death – from Plato to Novalis, Schopenhauer, and Pieper   95
    Dan Farrelly

6 | Human Attitudes towards the Death of Animals   105
    Alan Baird

7 | Ignoring Death – War, Maps and Advertising   121
    Joseph Brady

8 | Brecht and Weill's *Berliner Requiem* as a Necropolitical Statement   147
    Wolfgang Marx

Contributors   169

Illustrations   172

Acknowledgements

A project like this book can only succeed with the support of many individuals and institutions. First and foremost among these was on this occasion Joseph Brady who deserves special praise as he not only contributed a chapter but also undertook the arduous process of typesetting the entire book. Furthermore I am most grateful to him and Alun Carr (UCD School of Mechanical and Material Engineering) for designing its cover. I would also like to thank Mary Broderick, Berni Metcalfe and Glenn Dunne from the National Library of Ireland as well as Kate Manning at the UCD Archives who all went out of their way in selecting photographs and making them available to us. Anne Boddaert (Crawford Gallery, Cork) and David Roe (Felix Rosenstiel's Widow & Son, London) were instrumental in granting us access to John Lavery's painting of Terence MacSwiney's funeral procession in Southwark Cathedral. Salvador Ryan (St Patrick's College, Maynooth) and Sarah Prescott (UCD College of Arts and Humanities) were most supportive of the project. Dan Farrelly and all at Carysfort Press deserve equally sincere thanks for their support. Last but not least I would like to thank all contributors for their patience during the lengthy gestation process of this volume.

Dublin, April 2017

Wolfgang Marx

Introduction

Wolfgang Marx

> Who telleth a tale of unspeaking death?
> Who lifteth the veil of what is to come?
> Who painteth the shadows that are beneath
> The wide-winding caves of the peopled tomb?
> Or uniteth the hopes of what shall be
> With the fears and the love for that which we see?[1]

Percy Bysshe Shelley, from *On Death*

'Who telleth a tale of unspeaking death?' With these words from his poem *On Death* Percy Bysshe Shelley expresses the speaker's dread in the face of death as all his knowledge is based on what we experience in this world while the 'secret things of the grave' cannot be anticipated. The line opens the fifth and last stanza in which the poem culminates in a series of rhetorical questions as quoted above. It seems obvious that the speaker does not expect a positive response: Death itself remains silent even once we come to occupy our tombs, and while everybody has knowledge of the things we can 'see' in this world (the poem's last word clings to the only reality the speaker seems to be certain of), there is nothing more than hope regarding what lies beyond it. We may of course rely on the solace offered by religious belief, but since faith cannot be proved through our senses this does not seem helpful to Shelley.

Yet there are other ways in which we can read this stanza's first line. If death itself really does not speak, how do we get to know all the stories, the legends, and the philosophical concepts related to it? The answer is: through the living. Death has been one of the biggest topics tackled by philosophers, priests, artists, writers and just about everybody else probably since human beings first became aware of their mortality. However, among the important questions posed by the existence of death is not just what may or may not happen to us once we have died, but also what someone else's death means to us as individuals and as members of communities. All societies have developed rites to provide consolation to those close to a deceased, to honour her / his memory and achievements, and to reaffirm individual and group identities that are challenged each time death strikes. This second volume of the *Dublin Death Studies* series engages mainly with ways in which death has been utilized – in some cases even instrumentalized – by the living in order to shape their own world (rather than speculate about the afterlife), either in order to confirm existing structures, values and belief systems, or to challenge them. How a politician, a writer or an artist dies often significantly influences the way in which we assess her or his work in hindsight, so that the tale of this person or that work keeps evolving.

The *Dublin Death Studies* series has grown out of the work of the interdisciplinary research project *Death, Burial and the Afterlife* which is based at University College Dublin's College of Arts and Humanities. Yet the eight new tales of unspeaking death collated here are not restricted to the disciplines united in that College; alongside essays representing art history, ethnomusicology, German studies, historical musicology and history there are contributions by a geographer, a sociologist and a veterinary scientist. The result is a truly interdisciplinary dialogue that focuses on research undertaken recently at University College Dublin. The essays were written by four current and two retired UCD academics, as well as two recent UCD PhD graduates who now pursue careers elsewhere.

The first four tales focus on individual deaths and funerals while the book's second half engages with more general questions related to how individuals and society think about (or are hoped to think about) death. In 'Illustrious Corpses: Burying Irish Nationalist Heroes' Michael Laffan analyses a special type of funeral in Ireland, that of political and nationalist heroic figures, commencing with Thomas Davis in 1845 and Daniel O'Connell in 1847 and concluding with the re-interment of Thomas Kent in 2015. A recurring characteristic of these was the appropriation of the dead heroic character by nationalist movements or parties, often at the expense of the wishes of their families or the church. Sometimes different groups even competed with each other for the opportunity to use a famous corpse as a figurehead furthering their respective goals, more than once deceiving the authorities or even displaying downright criminal behaviour. Laffan describes in detail the (in hindsight sometimes almost comedic) events surrounding the funerals of public figures like Parnell, O'Donovan Rossa, Collins, MacSwiney, Higgins, Stagg or the repatriation of Casement's remains. In every single case the dead were instrumentalized as representations of a certain identity, culture or ideology, often one which was in the process of being constructed at the time. The dead are not so much grieved for or honoured for their own sake but are rather turned into a symbol furthering a much bigger cause.

The second tale focuses on death in Ireland as well, yet from a very different perspective. In 'Crying by Singing Out: Performing the Cry-die of North West Cameroon in Dublin' Sheryl Lynch looks at the funeral rites of one of the many immigrant communities in Ireland, namely those of the Grassfield people from an English-speaking area in the otherwise Francophone Cameroon. Lynch has studied their traditional mortuary ritual, the so-called 'cry-die', in Cameroon and compares it to its rendition among a small emigré community in the Irish capital. Detailed descriptions of the structure of the music are accompanied by an analysis of its functions within different social spaces at home and in the European diaspora, not least of which is the strengthening of cultural identity among those living abroad. This ritual combines older traditional beliefs with newer forms of social performance while also leaving space for the personal responses of the bereaved. Unlike the funeral processions, speeches and memorials discussed in Michael Laffan's chapter, the cry-die addresses no outside spectators but focuses on the mutual relationships of the participants and the deceased – yet both types of events have proved equally important for the shaping and developing of group identities.

While the first two chapters demonstrate how the living derive meaning and strengthen their identity from the rites related to death and burial, the following two essays discuss how the interaction of the life and works of human beings shapes their post-mortem image. Corinna Ricasoli's topic is Pietro da Cortona, an important early Baroque artist and member of the *Accademia di San Luca* (the association of painters in Rome) who spent decades reconstructing the *Accademia's* church of Santi Luca e Martina before being buried there after his death in 1669. Ricasoli regards not just his tomb but the church as a whole as Pietro's most lasting monument. Beginning with his tenure as president of the *Accademia* (1634-36) and, partly at his own expense, Pietro planned and supervised significant building works in the church, having it in mind as his own burial place from the beginning. But he was not unopposed – Ricasoli outlines in detail the intrigues between Pietro and (after his death) his followers and members of the *Accademia* about jurisdiction over sections of the church, access to the crypt, the positioning of memory tablets and other details that show that the other painters were not willing to surrender 'their' church easily to Pietro's rule, or let it become his burial monument. Ricasoli's research shows that only knowledge of these historic developments and the study of the resulting artistic monument together give us a full picture of the artist that was Pietro da Cortona.

In 'How Tocqueville became "Tocqueville". Gustave de Beaumont's Letters from Cannes and the First Edition of *Memoir, Letters, and Remains of Alexis de Tocqueville*', Andreas Hess illuminates another example of the interaction between biographical details and the afterlife-view of a person's artistic or intellectual achievements, with the way in which a life unfolded (or, in this case, concluded) shaping how it was to be evaluated in hindsight. Gustave de Beaumont was a close collaborator and friend of Alexis de Tocqueville and spent much time witnessing the political theorist's slow, drawn-out decline from tuberculosis in spring 1859. Subsequently Beaumont played a crucial role in shaping the picture the world acquired of Tocqueville as an iconic political thinker. Expanding theories by Dominik Bartmanski and Jeffrey Alexander, Hess argues that Beaumont's 'lived experience' of his friend's decline played a crucial part in his project of 'icon construction'. He depicted Tocqueville as a man whose considerable achievements were not based on superhuman abilities, but were instead reached despite his very human limitations, making those achievements appear even more extraordinary. Three years after his friend's death Beaumont published a book which combined a memoir with some of Tocqueville's writings, thus highlighting the equal relevance of a personal, morally outstanding life and a significant contribution to intellectual discourse to Tocqueville's iconic standing.

With the fifth chapter we leave the engagement with dying or dead individuals behind and move on to more general and fundamental questions regarding our understanding of death. Dan Farrelly's 'Philosophical Reflections on Reality and Death – From Plato to Novalis, Schopenhauer, and Pieper' outlines the German Catholic philosopher Josef Pieper's views of death. He describes Pieper's concept of the *mirandum* – the sense of wonderment we feel when encountering something positively awe-inspiring and overwhelming – as something beyond our normal world of representations accessible to the senses. It points towards the idealist's Platonic world of 'ultimate reality' – which is not dissimilar to death in that death too represents a transition to a different world. While there is no proof of the existence of that world, there is also none that refutes it. But, as Pieper explains with reference to Socrates's attitude during his final hours in prison (when he refused the option to flee and drank the chalice filled with hemlock): those being truthful, just and brave have nothing to fear from death.

While Josef Pieper's thinking is based on philosophical and theological traditions, Alan Baird chooses a scientific approach when discussing 'Human Attitudes towards the Death of Animals'. He regards humans as 'just another species' that differs from other animals in their advanced brain development, yet is otherwise very similar to them as, biologically speaking, the death of animals is characterized by the cessation of the same processes. While this has always been the case, man's view of animals has changed over time. We usually regard animals as belonging to one of a specific range of categories and treat them accordingly: friends (pets), tools (horses, but also food animals), vermin, demons and imaginary animals. Baird shows how these different categories may change radically over time, when for example cats that had undergone the elaborate death ritual of mummification in ancient Egypt were later used as fertiliser in Victorian England. Religions differ on whether or not animals may have a soul and can experience an afterlife. Given the biological and genetic similarities between homo sapiens and animals, questions such as those concerning the soul and the awareness of death (or a potential afterlife) in animals are just as much (if not more) based on changes in human attitudes than in observable facts.

The last two chapters are dedicated to war, an event always causing mass death and suffering – but to very different aspects of it. As Joseph Brady points out in 'Ignoring Death – War, Maps and Advertising', despite its horrors war has always fascinated people. But for this fascination to work, a very selective reception had to occur, one that focused on individual deeds of heroism and bravery, on overcoming odds stacked against oneself. War can be seen as an opportunity to demonstrate a commitment to a higher cause and overcome selfishness. But this approach usually comes with a near-total exclusion of the costs of war, of the destruction it causes and the lives it costs. It seems unthinkable that marketing executives would see war as an advertising opportunity, yet this is what happened during the First and, especially, during the Second World War. Businesses sought to capitalize upon this sanitized image of war as a wholly noble and heroic activity and they found that the map was the means to do it. Maps conveyed much useful information about the progress of the war but they could also carry an advertising message. Map publishers produced maps in all formats with customized advertisements that linked particular businesses with the noble activity of war. The message was clear – 'war is heroic and noble, these companies support the war so you should support these companies both during and after the war has ended'. Death was virtually absent from these maps, and if suffering was indicated (such as a city in flames after a bombing raid) it was inevitably associated with the enemy. This use of war to increase a company's profits may leave the reader with some ethical questions.

The final chapter engages with a musical response to war, interpreting 'Brecht and Weill's *Berliner Requiem* as a Necropolitical Statement'. Necropolitics, a postcolonial concept introduced by Achille Mbembe, regards the power to decide who can stay alive and who has to die as a state's (or a ruler's) ultimate expression of power. War can thus be described as a necropolitical act which condemns large numbers of people (including many of the state's own citizens) to a premature death. Based on a selection of Brecht's poems and set to Weill's equally fascinating and thought-provoking music, the *Berliner Requiem*'s bleak and uncompromising text addresses directly the horrors of death, the decomposition of bodies, the social death due to being forgotten by the living – issues not just affecting soldiers but also many civilians, as exemplified by the two women who are the subjects of two of the Requiem's movements. Written for a radio broadcast, the piece was aimed at the working and lower-middle classes – those that usually do not engage with art music –, and Weill carefully tailored it for this purpose. Brecht and Weill didn't want to depress their listeners but rather wished to set a thought process in motion that might help them in realising that they were at the receiving end of the often negative necropolitical decisions of the ruling classes, and that something might need to be done about this. The *Berliner Requiem* thus represents an approach as far away as possible from the death-ignoring war maps serving as marketing tools.

In recent times death has become a favourite topic among Irish intellectuals, with Fin Dwyer's *1348: A Medieval Apocalypse – The Black Death in Ireland*, Lisa Marie Griffith and Ciarán Wallace's *Grave Matters. Death and Dying in Dublin, 1500 to the Present* and Salvador Ryan's *Death and the Irish: A Miscellany* all being published in 2016. We hope that *Who telleth a tale of unspeaking death?* will add a distinctive voice to this discourse as our eight tales offer new insights into how people of different times and cultures cope with death, make sense of others' lives and their achievements through it, and sometimes use it to push their own agendas – all phenomena that are we can still observe today, not least during the Irish decade of commemorations.

---

[1] Percy Bysshe Shelley, 'On Death', in *The Oxford Book of Death*, ed. D. J. Enright (Oxford: Oxford University Press, 1983), 2.

1 | Illustrious Corpses: Burying Irish Nationalist Heroes

Michael Laffan

The most famous of all Irish short stories is James Joyce's 'The Dead'. The proclamation of an independent Irish Republic in 1916 began with the words 'In the name of God and of the dead generations'. Death, and the dead, have traditionally received more attention and respect in Ireland than in many other societies. It has been remarked that 'life in Ireland has long been troubled by the recurrent, insistent, ceremonious invocation of the dead'.[1] This study will examine some of the ways in which groups of Irish nationalists have used corpses and funerals as means of commemoration; as expressions of identity; as a method of inventing certain Irish traditions, and of creating imagined Irish communities; as a way of marginalizing or banishing rivals; and as weapons against not only British rulers, but also, more recently, against the governments of the independent Irish state.

As Graham Greene remarked in one of his novels, people are generally seen at their best at funerals.[2] They are important in Irish social life and many people prefer them to weddings; the crowds are larger and less regimented, and the atmosphere is more democratic. Even in the twenty-first century, funerals are still often followed by wakes. They are accompanied not only by grief and mourning, but by celebration of a person's life, of life itself, and of the water of life: whiskey. The throngs that gather to pay their last respects tend to be enormous by the standards that are common in many other countries. It is one of the few respects in which there may be some truth in the frequent and sometimes tiresome claim that the Irish are really a Mediterranean people who were cut adrift and who ended up several hundred miles further north than their natures had intended. One Polish observer has referred to Irish 'thanatophilia'.[3] Funerals are a final public display of one's position in the community, and the poor have been concerned that, at least in their coffins, they could keep up appearances. Some of them joined burial clubs, co-operative societies which ensured that people secured respectable burials after making regular small payments.[4] Macbeth might say of Duncan 'after life's fitful fever he sleeps well' but in Ireland death is not the end; the corpse cannot yet relax, and one final test still lies ahead: it has one last public performance, one more opportunity to lap up recognition and respect, and it can still inquire anxiously 'will I put on a good show? Will I draw a large crowd?'

Political funerals can be competitive and ruthless occasions. Rival groups claim kinship, try to exclude one another, or demand rights of succession. Bodies can be snatched, political wills can be overturned, and legacies can be diverted. The dead, their memory, and their cult can be powerful weapons in helping to shape national consciousness, and to create – or to undermine – allegiances. They help to consolidate identity, to link past and present, to annex a convenient image or reputation – and to prevent it from being stolen by rivals.

Of course there is nothing new or uniquely Irish about such patterns. Nearly two and a half millennia ago Ptolemy stole the body of Alexander the Great to legitimize his claim to control of Egypt, and medieval saints' remains were manufactured and multiplied to meet the importunate demands of pious believers. Eva Perón's body had a varied and much-travelled existence for two decades after her death. The constant refurbishment of Lenin, the removal of Stalin from the mausoleum on Red Square, and the reburial of the czar's family, show that Russian rulers' influence does not end in their first grave. In 1989 the reinterment of Imre Nagy in Budapest was a prelude to the collapse of Communism. There are many more examples. But the Irish have shown a particular obsession with the afterlife of their heroes. Death is frequently no more than the beginning of a new phase – and in some instances, a far more interesting phase – in a patriot's career.

In nineteenth and early twentieth century Ireland funerals and related commemorations were often the best – and sometimes the only – means whereby the oppressed and defeated could express their alienation and dissent. They could be a voice of the powerless. The bodies of great or symbolic figures were useful because they aroused people's emotions or (on certain occasions) because their burial enabled radicals to meet in public at times when meetings other than funerals might be banned. They could link an unworthy present to a heroic past, or attach a contemporary figure to a noble tradition – normally one of resistance and rebellion. Irish nationalists could make 'political speeches in graveyards in search of endorsement from people too dead to demur'.[5] They could point out to the authorities that 'you may have the power, but we represent the nation; you control the present, but we represent the past'. And many would have shared the sentiments of the party slogan coined by George Orwell in *Nineteen-Eighty-Four*: 'who controls the past controls the future: who controls the present controls the past'.[6]

In Ireland as elsewhere 'national myths do not arise spontaneously from people's actual experiences. They are something which people acquire from someone else ... it is not a question of the people constantly remembering: they remember because someone is constantly reminding them'.[7] Funerals were an ideal method of reminding the Irish people of past or present grievances, of fighting complacency and acquiescence. The old Fenian John O'Leary remarked that we cannot all be heroes, but we can all be hero-worshippers. And funerals provided occasions for such hero-worship – for mass involvement, for release of emotions such as sorrow and anger – and also for a 'day out'. They, and similar occasions, were often accompanied by a 'feel-good factor'. In June 1898, at a ceremony at Wolfe Tone's grave, Underwood O'Connell from the United States declared that Tone 'exemplified in his life and labours one of the greatest and most solid doctrines of the Catholic Church. The Catholic Church taught that love of country was next to the love of God (cheers)'. Then he provided his audience with even better news: in honouring the memory of Wolfe Tone they honoured themselves.[8]

Funerals also often took the form of a sort of fashion show, and various groups that had had little or no connection with the dead hero paraded along the streets like models on a catwalk. At the unveiling of the O'Connell statue in Dublin there was admiration for the imposing appearance of 2,000 coal porters, who had been known in the old days of agitation as 'O'Connell's Body Guard'. They carried a large banner, borne on a carriage drawn by four horses. On it stood a life-sized figure of O'Connell against a green background, surmounted by a crown and surrounded by shamrocks, while a smaller banner included a pair of stout porters, shovels in hand. According to one account 'the painters were decidedly the most numerous as they were amongst the most intelligent of the various handicrafts ... The stewards comprised some of the most influential employers of the "gentle craft", as well as the humbler but not less respectable operatives. They all wore handsome green and white rosettes, with gold lace trimmings'.[9] There were many such reports; clearly the craftsmen and tradesmen of Dublin enjoyed flaunting their splendour. (On a later occasion a complaint was made about groups who took part in such processions 'merely for the sake of advertising and exploiting themselves'.[10])

Political funerals also attracted welcome recognition. Lists of those present in processions behind the coffin normally gave prominence to Irish-Americans, or to others from abroad – in this respect modelling themselves on royal or other state funerals where representatives of foreign governments were given places of honour. It was as if Irish nationalists wished to stress that we are not alone; we have friends in the outside world. The admission of a French observer at O'Connell's funeral in 1847 was noted proudly: Irish grief and devotion surpassed that of the French nation when Napoleon's remains had been returned from St Helena seven years earlier.[11]

Political factions felt obliged not only to stake their claim over an appropriate corpse. They had also to keep rivals at bay. Funerals were competitive sports, and on every appropriate occasion comparisons were drawn with past events; claims that a procession was the biggest gathering in Dublin since the funeral of O'Connell, or Parnell, or Collins, were journalistic commonplaces.

O'Connell

By the early nineteenth century a pattern had already been established; for example, when Thomas Davis died in 1845, despite his unionist family's wishes for a private funeral, the streets were thronged with carriages and pedestrians that followed the hearse.[12] But like so much else in nationalist Ireland, grand-scale political funerals began with Daniel O'Connell. He was the dominant figure of his generation, 'the Liberator' who inspired, organized and politicized the Irish masses. He had been deeply concerned with his appearance – he devoted considerable care to his clothes, he was conscious of getting fat, and his unhappiness at his loss of hair led him to wear a dark, curly wig even in his 70s, long after wigs had gone out of fashion. Perhaps understandably in view of his weight problems he worried about the solidity of the platforms on which he would stand, and he instructed his followers to ensure that he spoke with the wind behind him.[13] It was appropriate that his funeral in 1847 should receive the same attention that he had devoted to planning his great public meetings. This was facilitated by the fact that he died in Genoa and his coffin did not reach Ireland for three months; but even then the funeral group was obliged to wait a few days in Chester before sailing on its last lap because preparations in Dublin had not yet been completed.

By any standards it was a splendid affair. A mere thirteen years after the first railway line had been opened on the island special trains were provided to bring mourners to and from Dublin.[14] Crowds marched by his house and along a circuitous route through the city centre to the new cemetery in Glasnevin. The preparations were detailed; for example the sequence in the procession was laid down as being the lord mayor, archbishops, bishops, clergy, nobility, judges and members of the bar, the high sheriff, the undersecretary, the attorney general, the solicitor general, members of the House of Commons, and gentry. Fifty trades were represented, in an order that they decided among themselves, with the result that the paper-stainers came first and the nailers last.

O'Connell was compared, perhaps improbably in some cases, to Demosthenes, Hannibal, Scipio Africanus, Julius Caesar, Cicero,

Constantine, Charlemagne, King John Sobieski and Napoleon.[15] For a man of his European reputation this might make sense, at least in its broad outlines, but the lack of Irish models would form a contrast to all later such occasions. The Catholic Church seized the occasion to turn him into a defender of the faith; his nationalism and his radicalism were conveniently forgotten. (And although not a revolutionary he was a radical; for example, he was a passionate opponent of American slavery and a supporter of Jewish as well as Catholic Emancipation.) A few years later, when his body was moved to its present position at the foot of an enormous round tower in Glasnevin cemetery, the Dominican Fr Burke praised him in terms more appropriate to a saint than to a politician. 'Obedience to the Church's laws, quick zeal for her honour and the dignity of her worship; a spirit of penance refining whilst it expiated, chastening whilst it ennobled, all that was natural in the man; constant and frequent use of the Church's sacraments, which shed the halo of grace around his head – these were the last grand lessons which he left to his people, and thus did the sun of his life set in the glory of Christian holiness.'[16]

Fenians and Others

But already the Church's role had been challenged. Perhaps the most bizarre Irish political funeral was that of Terence Bellew McManus in 1861, and it (rather than O'Connell's) provided the prototype that would be followed in future. It formed the climax to what has been described as 'the grandfather of Irish wakes', since the ceremonies began eleven months earlier on the shores of the Pacific, and proceeded from San Francisco through Panama (overland in those days) and New York to Queenstown and Dublin. McManus was one of the more improbable members of the Irish patriotic pantheon. He was a relatively insignificant member of the Young Ireland movement who was imprisoned for his part in the 1848 rebellion, escaped, and fled to the United States. He lived there quietly and died soon afterwards, after an incident 'while in his cups'. He was buried in San Francisco and his friends decided to place a memorial over his grave. Gradually this idea developed until it was transformed into a far more grandiose scheme: his body should be sent 'home'. Californian Fenians took over control of the operation, and when the secretary of the rival Hibernians inquired about the opinions of the McManus family he was informed that they could make no possible objection, since all of Ireland wanted the reburial. They dug him up and transported him back to a country from which he had been barred in his lifetime.[17]

When news reached Dublin that his coffin was on the way the Fenians displayed their formidable organizational skills. They established a funeral committee and carefully excluded McManus's former Young Ireland comrades – who were dismissed as unacceptably moderate. (They had also been excluded from O'Connell's funeral fourteen years earlier.) One of this group complained that they were 'in danger of being repulsed from following their old comrade's hearse unless they followed as satellites of someone in a mask'.[18] The bishop of Cork would not allow honours to be paid in his diocese to someone associated with a secret society, so McManus's body rested in Queenstown cathedral, where the bishop was more flexible. In Dublin Archbishop Cullen was also unsympathetic, and the lying in state took place in the Mechanics' Institute.

On the night before McManus's funeral the priest who had been designated to give the panegyric was vetted by the Fenians and rejected on the grounds that his remarks were 'aspirational', rather than full-bloodedly revolutionary. In Dublin a funeral car bearing a pyramid-shaped cenotaph was followed by a vast crowd, which included the near-obligatory Irish-American delegation – placed immediately behind the funeral carriage. Everyone in the procession wore a band of black crepe on his left arm, the passage was kept clear by horsemen armed with batons, and the proceedings revealed an almost military discipline. Its route passed hallowed buildings associated with Irish history, particularly with rebel heroes, and the pattern of a via dolorosa was established. To organize a funeral on a scale that could rival that of the great O'Connell, despite Church hostility, and for a person who had been virtually unknown before his death, was a formidable achievement. (A contrast could be made with the funeral some years earlier of the Duke of Wellington, the greatest hero of nineteenth century Britain. Even though two months had elapsed between his death and his burial, allowing for detailed preparations, everything that could go wrong did go wrong.[19])

Moderate nationalists could be just as ruthless as the Fenians in taking over a valuable corpse. When Charles Stewart Parnell died suddenly in Brighton his followers dashed there from London, seized his body, and arranged that it should be transported back to Dublin for another spectacular funeral. In their confident haste it had not even occurred to them that, since Parnell had belonged to the Church of Ireland, a Protestant ceremony might be appreciated by his family. A brief Anglican service in St Michan's church was added later. As his body lay in state black fabric was draped across the pillars in imitation of the Pantheon in

Paris during Gambetta's funeral a few years earlier. (An observer remarked caustically that 'it can scarcely be said that its effect was artistic, but beyond all doubt it was eminently striking'.[20]) Hurlers carried their camáns on their shoulders, adorned with green ribbons – even though Parnell was a cricket player who loathed the colour green. His funeral procession passed over O'Connell Bridge, and through the streets of Dublin (Fig. 1.1).[21] He was buried with great pomp. However two weeks after his death his sister Anna wrote a forceful letter to *The Irish Times* pointing out that while Parnell did not think much of religious beliefs he did think highly of his ancestors, and he would have preferred to be buried either with them, or else where he had died. She then mentioned the claim 'that my brother's body belonged to the Irish people' and continued 'that is true if the fact of their having killed him gave them a title to it'.[22] But soon everyone claimed him, and his grave was visited by figures as varied as the revolutionary leader James Stephens and Edward, Prince of Wales.

Fig. 1.1) Charles Stewart Parnell's funeral procession crossing O'Connell Bridge in Dublin.

In organizing a patriotic funeral it helped to have a great leader, such as O'Connell or Parnell; others, such as McManus or (in 1915) O'Donovan Rossa, were chosen because they were available at the right time. Bodies were useful for funerals, but they were not necessary, and organizers could arrange a perfectly satisfactory ceremony without one. In 1867 the 'Manchester Martyrs' were hanged in Salford and their bodies buried in quicklime. These executions caused outrage throughout nationalist Ireland, and in the absence of authentic martyred corpses dozens of funerals were held throughout the country. In Dublin, for example, it was estimated that as many as 30,000 people marched in procession behind a hearse bearing three empty black coffins with the sacred names of 'Allen', 'Larkin' and 'O'Brien'. Brass bands played the funeral march from *Saul*.[23] Similar rituals were enacted throughout the country.

Perhaps the most remarkable of all such events took place in 1898. The grand ceremony began with a procession through nationalist Belfast, and this was followed by transportation to Dublin, and two nights' lying in state at the site of the old Newgate prison. Then the commemoration began in earnest. Once more thousands of people took a circuitous route through the centre of the city, passing Tone's birthplace, the building where his body lay after his death, and the site of Emmet's execution, needing three hours to cover three miles until it reached its final resting place. And all this, not for a hero, or even for a nobody, but for a lump of rock – the granite foundation stone for a monument to Wolfe Tone.[24] The site was subsequently moved and the statue was not erected for another 68 years. (Such processions past symbolic buildings formed part of an international pattern; in Paris, for example, political funerals were expected to include in their routes one of the sites of power – the Bourbon, Luxembourg or Élysée palace.[25])

If people could be buried in absentia, as with the Manchester Martyrs, they could also attend in absentia. In 1917 Archbishop Walsh of Dublin wrote to the organizers of Thomas Ashe's funeral – in a letter which was published in the newspapers – 'I feel it a duty to take part in the public protest ... Kindly say to what place I should send my car so that it can most conveniently find its place in the procession'. His car, with drawn blinds, duly took its place immediately after the chief mourners. The archbishop himself, however, watched from the presbytery window of the church at Arran Quay as the procession, including his own car, passed by.[26]

The Church was normally treated with respect, and if its support could not be obtained, at least its neutrality should be secured. Traditionally it insisted on peaceful and democratic measures in the present, but it was prepared to bless rebellions that were safely in the past and that could not challenge the existing social or political order. (One clear, vivid example comes from a mosaic in Galway Cathedral, which was constructed in Sienese Gothic style in the mid 1960s. It features Christ rising from the tomb, and on both sides are cameos of two Catholic martyrs – to the left, one of the leaders of the Easter Rising, P. H. Pearse, and to the right, John F. Kennedy. It was a product of its time.) Nationalists knew that if possible the Church should be disarmed, appeased, or – ideally – incorporated. Even in the case of the Fenian-organized McManus funeral, which was repudiated by the Catholic archbishop of Dublin, prominent in the lists of those present was a member of the Papal brigade who had fought for Pius IX against Garibaldi. Whatever might be the pattern in Italy, in Ireland republicans could be devout Catholics.

The Revolutionary Years

The rhetoric of radical nationalism often took religious forms, and in his oration at Rossa's funeral Pearse's language was Biblical or liturgical: 'here by the grave of this unrepentant Fenian, we renew our baptismal vows ... Let no man blaspheme the cause that the dead generations of Ireland served ... This is a place of peace, sacred to the dead ... I hold it a Christian thing ... to hate evil ... Our foes ... cannot undo the miracles of God'. No-one could confuse Irish republican revolutionaries with their anti-clerical or atheistic counterparts on the European Continent. Walsh facilitated the funerals of rebel figures such as Rossa, Thomas Ashe and Terence MacSwiney, while keeping a careful distance after the death of the moderate constitutionalist John Redmond, some of whose policies he had deplored; 'he elevated the legacy of physical force men'.[27]

Some prominent nationalists were buried with little pomp; John Mitchel's obsequies 'were carried out in the simplest and most unostentatious manner', although it was claimed nonetheless that at least 10,000 people were present.[28] There was only a brief graveside oration when Stephens died in 1901. John O'Leary did not want his funeral to turn into a national demonstration, yet it attracted a large crowd.[29] Characteristically, Michael Davitt chose a simple, private funeral in his native Mayo. But circumstances and opportunities ensured that political funerals became fashionable once more, even if their details changed.

By 1915, after the formation of two (later three) rival paramilitary forces in Ireland, and after the outbreak of the World War, the funeral of O'Donovan Rossa was a military occasion – although Arthur Griffith wrote that 'his body was borne through the streets of Dublin as the body of a saint might be borne by his people'.[30] Perhaps like McManus, Rossa was a strange choice. In his oration Pearse described him as 'this unrepentant Fenian', but he provoked controversy in the republican movement. Many radical nationalists thought him a pathetic figure and a buffoon. It was even claimed that he had endorsed Redmond and the war effort, although his family dismissed this as untrue.[31] Tom Clarke, who stage-managed the impressive ceremonies surrounding the funeral, remarked that 'if Rossa had planned to die at the most opportune moment for serving his country, he could not have done better'.[32]

His funeral provided not only an example of 'the dead hand of the past', but it was also an oratorical incitement to future violence – against a British administration that was characterized by its laxity and tolerance. 'Volunteers' armed with rifles, accompanied by cavalry, marched in disciplined fashion through the streets. After P. H. Pearse's inflammatory speech – which ended with the incantation 'the fools, the fools, the fools, they have left us our Fenian dead, and while Ireland holds these graves Ireland unfree shall never be at peace' – a volley of shots was fired over the grave. In many respects the funeral was a rehearsal for the Easter Rising. Together with those of O'Connell, McManus and Parnell, it 'established the rhetorical and ritual framework for the messianic style of nationalist remembrance'.[33]

Fig. 1.2) A volley of shots is fired at the funeral of Thomas Ashe.
Courtesy of the National Library of Ireland.

Two years later, when Thomas Ashe died as a result of forced feeding while on a hunger strike, radical nationalists were able to gather and show their strength for the first time since the rebellion. Volunteers controlled the streets, and the hitherto unknown Michael Collins appeared in public for the first time. After shots had been fired he made the briefest of orations: 'nothing additional remains to be said. That volley which we have just heard is the only speech which is proper to make above the grave of a dead Fenian' (Fig. 1.2). The time for talk was over. New technology was exploited on this occasion; one newspaper reported that details of the funeral were filmed and shown in a cinema that night – thereby revealing 'what Dublin enterprise can do in the "movie world"'.[34]

The British authorities were approached warily; even in the case of funerals, they could impose damaging restrictions or make harmful interventions. But everyone knew that, in contrast to all other nationalist demonstrations, the hands of the authorities were tied by their knowledge that funerals could not be banned. With few exceptions they behaved with restraint and forbearance.

It was in the aftermath of the Easter Rising of 1916 that the pattern of commemoration, and of British repression, reached their climax. Long processions of mourners and sympathizers followed coffins and – particularly when martial law was imposed – honouring the dead was virtually the only circumstance in which large gatherings could be held. The most spectacular of these was the funeral of Terence MacSwiney, the lord mayor of Cork, who died on hunger strike in England in October 1920 (Fig. 1.3). The funeral ceremonies began in Southwark Cathedral and passed through the streets of London, but his body was not allowed to enter Dublin, and the British government provided a ship that sailed directly from Holyhead to Cork.[35] The army imposed restrictions on the funeral procession – such as a general guideline that it should not stretch for more than a quarter of a mile (or 400 metres). Archbishops, bishops and over a hundred priests took part, and the arrangements were entirely in the hands of the Irish Volunteers/IRA. Politicians, priests and soldiers combined in an act of defiance towards British rule, and in the circumstances of the time no comparable form of protest would have been possible.

Continuities

The Anglo-Irish Treaty brought about major changes, but some patterns endured and rival groups of Irish nationalists continued their old quarrels. These feuds often took the form of struggles over the inheritance from the past, over the right to claim succession to the aims, methods or

Fig. 1.3) Terence MacSwiney's funeral procession in London. Courtesy of UCD Archives.

images of dead heroes. Radical republicans, who were unwilling to accept the compromise settlement with Britain, portrayed themselves as the only legitimate successors of earlier rebels – and compromisers were traitors to the past as well as to the present.

The Treaty split and the Civil War resulted in rival sets of funerals. The two founding fathers of the Irish Free State, Arthur Griffith and Michael Collins, died within ten days of one another. Griffith was buried with, in the words of one newspaper account, 'a manifestation of sorrow not by a party or by a section, but with the restraint and dignity befitting a Government and a people'. A hundred postmen marched in the procession, one of them carrying his postbag.[36] Griffith was solid and prosaic; he inspired respect, not veneration, and his colleagues shared his worthy virtues.

Even though Collins had been head of the provisional government he was buried as a soldier. When the coffin arrived at City Hall almost all the pallbearers were generals, either major-general, commandant-general or plain general.[37] In the funeral procession, which made its way slowly via O'Connell Street to Glasnevin, soldiers came first, then priests, followed

Fig 1.4) Funeral procession of Michael Collins, Dublin, O'Connell Street. Courtesy of the National Library of Ireland.

by more soldiers, members of the headquarters staff, the chief mourners, intimate friends, and only then members of the government and of the Dáil (Fig. 1.4). The oration was given by Richard Mulcahy, now minister for defence but until recently the army chief of staff. He described the dead commander as 'a hero and a legend', and Bishop Fogarty who gave the panegyric declared that if Collins had lived in the Middle Ages 'he would have been a coeur de lion, a knight of endless and dazzling romance ... Inevitably we recall the history of Joan of Arc. She appeared suddenly, did her work for France, and disappeared almost in a day'.[38] But it was Griffith's funeral, and not Collins's so soon afterwards, that set the commemorative pattern for future Irish governments.[39]

The republicans Cathal Brugha and Harry Boland were killed early in the civil war, and their funerals were attended by large numbers of followers. Brugha's widow made it clear that she did not wish any government representatives or officials to attend, while Collins wrote 'I'd send a wreath but I suppose they'd return it torn up'.[40] But some chivalry remained. During Boland's funeral government troops laid down their arms, removed their caps, and stood to attention as the procession passed by.[41]

In 1924 the Free State authorities released the remains of 77 republicans who had been shot during the civil war. Government troops attended many of the re-burials, and in Dundalk their efforts to prevent republicans firing shots over the graves resulted in gunfire and a stampede in the course of which many people suffered minor injuries.[42]

Some years later a 'double' pair of funerals illustrated neatly the new divisions. Kevin O'Higgins, the deputy president, was assassinated in July 1927, and the state organized a dramatic funeral. The cortège was reported to be two miles long, and more wreaths were displayed than at any Dublin funeral except that of Collins.[43] Days later his opponent Countess Markievicz died. The mourners were denied use of public buildings and – as at the funerals of Brugha and Boland – large numbers of armed soldiers took up positions near the plot. The interment had to be postponed because the gravediggers insisted that union rules forbade them to carry out this task on a Sunday.[44] Unusually the funeral drew representation from both the rival anti-Treaty parties, Fianna Fáil and Sinn Féin.

Long before de Valera came to power democratically in 1932 he had drifted away from his association with armed opponents of the Irish government. But some of his republican colleagues remained loyal to the extremism that he had embraced briefly and uncharacteristically. They refused to recognize the Irish state (the 'partition statelet', in the words of a later Sinn Féin president Ruairí Ó Brádaigh), or its government, parliament or electorate. They maintained this attitude until the 1980s, but after the Second World War (during which many of them had supported Nazi Germany) they abandoned their earlier campaign against independent Ireland – which had been their principal target for two decades. They continued, however, to regard themselves as the only true, faithful republicans and to dismiss all others, Collins and the Treaty supporters in 1922, de Valera and his Fianna Fáil party in 1926, and further defectors in later years, as deluded agents of British imperialism.

In the 1950s the IRA launched a half-hearted and disastrous campaign against Northern Ireland, in the course of which two of its members were killed. The funerals of Sean South and Feargal O'Hanlon attracted large crowds, and shops and business premises on the funeral route often closed in sympathy. In some cases the decision to do so was provoked by intimidation.

Independent Ireland continued to organize state funerals – for dignitaries as varied as the Fenian John Devoy in 1929, Eamon de Valera in 1975, and Garret FitzGerald in 2011. But these were formal, conventional occasions, and they attracted little or none of the passion and controversy associated with 'opposition' commemorations. Some, like the funeral of Charles Haughey in 2006, aroused far less public interest than the authorities had expected.

The state also commemorated its own violent origins in a restrained fashion. For several decades military parades were held at Easter to honour the 1916 Rising, although the pattern was discontinued between 1970 and 2006. Periodically wreaths were laid and speeches were made at the graves of dead heroes. It was advisable to have met a violent end; those such as O'Connell who had short-sightedly died in their beds failed to attract comparable attention. De Valera and his successors, members of democratic governments that felt themselves responsible to both parliament and people, knew that the effective independence achieved in 1922 – subsequently consolidated in further stages – was in large part the result of violence, of the resort to force between 1916 and 1921.

In many cases this provoked a degree of embarrassment. Some politicians gave the impression that they would have preferred the state to have had different origins, and they were careful to draw a line – 1921, 1926, 1932; the precise year varied from individual to individual and from party to party – after which violence that they endorsed in earlier decades or centuries was deemed unsuitable to new and happier circumstances. (Perhaps appropriately, their attitude was similar to that taken by the Catholic Church.) They feared a challenge from extreme republicans, from those IRA and Sinn Féin members who, in de Valera's words, 'continued on in that organisation which we have left [and] can claim exactly the same continuity that we claimed up to 1925'.[45] Such elements must be denied any opportunity to claim a monopoly of rights of descent, of succession, of legitimacy. To be accepted as the true heirs of the patriotic rebels who had inspired the founders of the state would reinforce their claim to represent an abstract 'Ireland' – against the wishes of the Irish people. No-one could deny that they had some rights of succession. 'It seems reasonable to admit the claim of the Provisional IRA, together with the penumbra of fellow-travellers which surrounds it, as the true descendant of the unreconstructed Irish republican tradition of the mid-nineteenth century ... they have a legitimacy of sorts ... in politics you do not have to be illegitimate to be a bastard.'[46]

One consequence of this claim to succession was the intermittently farcical series of visits to the grave of Wolfe Tone, the 'father of Irish republicanism'. In the 1920s the pro-Treaty government, which had accepted the compromise settlement of the Free State and had thereby postponed (or in their enemies' words 'betrayed') the Republic, tried half-heartedly to honour him. When it lost power in 1932 its members abandoned their efforts, probably with relief. But de Valera and the 'political' republicans of Fianna Fáil, who had made the pilgrimage in opposition, maintained the tradition now that they were in power, and they had to face opposition from more radical, 'physical force' republicans. Every June rival delegations went to the cemetery to lay their wreaths and to make their speeches. (Only in 1981 did Fianna Fáil break the pattern. It had just lost office in a general election and it was so demoralized that the party leaders simply forgot to go; local party supporters turned up on the usual date, to find that none of the leaders were present. The leaders went a few months later, and as a result of this oversight the party's commemorations have ever since taken place in the autumn.[47])

Other old patterns continued – particularly in the form of further splits among the extreme republicans, which in turn resulted in Tone's grave receiving visits from rival delegations of Official Sinn Féin, Provisional Sinn Féin, Republican Sinn Féin, and so on. But such patterns are not unique to Ireland. The Mur des Fédérés in the Père Lachaise cemetery in Paris has regularly attracted visits from rival delegations of the equally fissiparous French Left.

From time to time the Irish state acted to preserve its revolutionary inheritance. In 1965 the remains of Roger Casement, who had been hanged and buried in London shortly after the Easter Rising, were exhumed and returned to Dublin. The British prime minister Harold

Wilson made discreet conditions; the authenticity of the bones could not be guaranteed with total certainty, but the Irish were to accept them in good faith. Casement must be reburied in the Republic – there could be no question of him being transferred to Northern Ireland – and 'sensational publicity' should be avoided. Wilson hoped to discuss these matters discreetly with the Taoiseach, Seán Lemass, if they should meet at Winston Churchill's funeral. Lemass, like President de Valera, felt unable to go to London on that occasion (some funerals were sacred but not others, and certainly not Churchill's). Nonetheless they reached agreement, and Lemass promised that Casement's remains would not be moved again until the unity of Ireland had been restored.[48]

The funeral was conducted with full military pomp and it was seen as a dress rehearsal for that of President de Valera (which did not take place for a further decade).[49] In contrast to the burials of so many imprisoned or executed Irish rebels in the past, this time the international representation was *official*; *The Irish Times* described how 'the Africans, Australians, Americans, men from Europe streamed up the aisle'.[50] But old struggles for influence continued. The first two wreaths to be laid beside the coffin were from the Sinn Féin party and the army council of the IRA. While crowds queued to pay their respects, 'the sound of brisker marching announced the arrival of 13 men who had been serving sentences on charges arising out of the disturbances which surrounded the visit of Princess Margaret and Lord Snowdon'. They had been released from prison the previous day, and now they came to lay a wreath – inscribed simply 'Political prisoners, Mountjoy'.[51] At the funeral de Valera illustrated a widespread attitude when he hoped that 'this grave, like the graves in Arbour Hill, like the grave at Bodenstown, the grave at Downpatrick, the grave in Templepatrick, and the grave at Greyabbey – this grave, like these others, will become a place of pilgrimage to which our young people will come and get renewed inspiration and renewed determination'.[52] By now many Irish people had grown out of such grave-worship, but not all.

A year later the state commemorated the fiftieth anniversary of the 1916 Easter Rising. The ceremonies, military and civilian, were on a grand and even triumphalist scale. But the most memorable and spectacular event of the celebrations was carried out by the 'anti-state', the IRA; it blew up Nelson's Pillar, the dominant feature of central Dublin.

The Shadow of the North

These events were almost the last acts in the age of innocence, the years when it was still possible to glorify past bloodshed without an awareness that a new cycle of violence had begun. The Northern 'troubles', which commenced in 1968-69, provoked a new round of confrontations between Dublin governments and Irish republicans. These took political, military and symbolic forms. The Irish state fought to prevent the Provisional IRA from staking its claim as the one true successor to patriotic opponents of British rule. Perhaps the most remarkable example of such conflict is the funerals of Frank Stagg – and here it is appropriate to use the plural, rather than the singular.

Stagg was an IRA hunger striker who died in England in February 1976. His remains were flown back to Ireland, and some members of his family waited for their arrival in Dublin airport – along with Ruairí Ó Brádaigh, the president of Sinn Féin, who carried a brown paper bag containing an Irish flag that he intended to place on the coffin. (Other family members, including his wife, were not present.) They were outraged to learn that the Irish government had ordered the plane to be diverted to Shannon airport, they denounced the government as 'body-snatchers', and they dashed there as quickly as possible. In Shannon the coffin was locked in the mortuary. It was then flown in an army helicopter to Stagg's native village in Mayo, and carried across fields and over a stone wall into the church. More than 1,000 soldiers and guards, dressed in anti-riot gear, patrolled the town of Ballina and the surrounding area. The church was virtually taken over by twenty guards who stood at the back and filled the two rows of benches nearest the coffin, while outside soldiers and two Panhard armoured cars controlled the crossroads. After dark, arc lights were powered by a mobile generator, and troops patrolled the surrounding fields. At the funeral the next day young men stoned the soldiers, who in turn fired rubber bullets. And all this was done to ensure that Stagg was buried in an 'ordinary' grave, and not in the 'Republican plot' nearby.[53] This grave was later covered with 40 cm of concrete, and the police maintained an around-the-clock surveillance for the next six months.

But this was just round one, or funeral number one. The government had commandeered a grave, but it had omitted to make any payment; with a brief exception in the 2000s, parsimony has been an enduring feature of Irish public life. Stagg's brother bought the plot (the government had forgotten to do so), and also the empty one beside it. One wet windy night in November 1977 a group of republicans spent hours digging down two metres in the empty, adjacent plot, and then tunnelled sideways until they reached Stagg's coffin. Scared that the concrete would fall on top of them, they removed the coffin, lifted it up, and carried it the short distance to the republican plot. There it was accompanied by an informal guard of honour and re-interred in a freshly-dug new grave. A symbolic shot was fired, and republicans could claim the final victory.[54] Dead bodies matter in Ireland.

Four years later, in 1981, the stakes were raised as, one by one, ten republican prisoners died on hunger strike. Their funerals became set-piece demonstrations of republican strength, anger, and manipulative skills; in the words of the leading authority on the subject, the ceremonies

> followed the same elaborate, stylized ritual: the funeral mass, the draping of the Irish Tricolour over the coffin, the funeral procession to the cemetery, the last volley, Lastpost, orders to pallbearers, orders to firing party, the flag on the coffin, gloves instead of army cap, the lone piper leading the procession, the funeral oration at the graveside – all of it awakened a deeper Catholic awareness of their own inner sense of historic victimization ... The funerals dissociated the IRA from the violence it inflicted ... exalted the dead, glorified their deeds, reaffirmed the cause for which they died, reburnished the glow of idealism, removed the tawdry and tarnished, gave existential affirmation to the permanence of the past.[55]

As had been the case with the Manchester Martyrs over a century earlier, or with the execution of the Easter Week rebel leaders, Irish nationalist opinion was aroused by what was widely seen as British brutality. As long as the British refrained from killing Irish people (or in 1981, as long as they avoided giving the impression that they were responsible for Irishmen's deaths) most Irish nationalists shunned the IRA and its allies. But now the republicans exploited sympathy with the hunger-strikers, they organized protest meetings, and they acquired invaluable publicity and goodwill. They made claims to an 'apostolic' succession; one particularly vivid example consists of a monument in the republican plot in Glasnevin cemetery, listing those who died on hunger strikes – starting with Thomas Ashe in 1917 and progressing through Terence MacSwiney and Frank Stagg to the 'ten men dead' of 1981. It is a simple and uncomplicated progression: one which links clearly the national struggle of 1917-21, in which Sinn Féin (and to a somewhat lesser extent, the IRA) was supported by the great mass of the Irish population, with the very different (and widely unpopular) campaign waged by a different IRA from the 1970s to the 1990s.

There were other lines of continuity. In every one of the ten tributes paid to the 1981 hunger-strikers they were placed in a wider context, linked with other acceptable figures in Irish or foreign history; with Tone, Pearse, MacSwiney, but also – perhaps improbably – with Gandhi and

Martin Luther King. The Iranian chargé d'affaires made a point of expressing 'international solidarity' and went to Belfast for the first of these funerals. Rhetoric moved with the times. Bobby Sands was described as being 'a symbol of hope for the unemployed, for the poor and oppressed, for the homeless, for those divided by partition', while Raymond McCreesh 'placed his body before the juggernaut of imperialism'.[56]

The Catholic Church continued to keep its distance. At some of the funerals in 1981 the officiating priests hedged their bets and blamed the British government, but time after time the columns of the republican paper *An Phoblacht* criticized the unsympathetic attitude and actions of the clergy. Bernadette McAliskey saw it as tragic that the Irish people, 'who for centuries have defended their church and their religion, should be, by and large, so sadly abandoned by it in their hour of greatest need'.[57]

But the absence of some funerals was a grim feature of the Northern conflict. Many of those who were murdered by the IRA were buried secretly, with the result that their families could not mourn them fully. Gradually over the years most of the bodies of these 'disappeared' were discovered, and they could at last be treated with an appropriate respect.

It was only when the ceasefires of 1994 and 1996 resulted in a dramatic fall in the number of violent deaths that voters – particularly in Northern Ireland but also to a much lesser extent in the Republic – began to support Sinn Féin in numbers that would have been inconceivable a decade earlier. The Good Friday agreement of 1998 gave Sinn Féin a new acceptance, and even legitimacy, in the eyes of some of those who used to regard it simply as 'the Murderers' Party'. (Many people still do.) This new respectability was neatly illustrated by the state funerals that took place in October 2001.

The Irish government decided to rebury ten IRA men who had been executed by the British in 1920-21. The timing provoked much cynicism, possibly fully deserved, because the ceremony took place on the morning after the Fianna Fáil party convention. The Taoiseach, Bertie Ahern, moved – not quite effortlessly – from one event to the other. People queried 'the seemingly ludicrous claim that, after eighty years, there was no other weekend available'.[58] An 'official' version of the origins of the state was inscribed on a plaque that accompanies the graves, and here we can see clearly an attempt to reclaim the War of Independence for the democratic Irish state; to stress that the IRA men who died in 1920-21 were soldiers in an army which was, at least in theory, acting on behalf of a democratically-elected parliament and government. It was an attempt to deny the legitimacy of all the later IRAs, which could make no such claim to democratic control. And accompanying Ahern and other political leaders, as an official honoured guest, was the Sinn Féin president, Gerry Adams, who only a few years before had committed himself to destroying the democratic state ruled from Dublin. He was now inside the tent. A few members of 'Continuity IRA' stood in the crowds that lined the streets outside the cemetery, but they were marginal figures.

In 2015 yet another such re-interment took place – of Thomas Kent, who had been executed in the aftermath of the Easter Rising, 99 years earlier. One critic described it as 'a necrophiliac, pomp-and-circumstance proceedings'.[59] Those who attended the funeral included the President, the Taoiseach, other political leaders, the British Ambassador, and the Papal Nuncio. But this event did not indicate a consensus in relation to the memory of past conflicts. When the state organized a 'decade of commemorations' to mark the centenary of the revolutionary years of 1912-23 the Sinn Féin party launched a rival 'national programme of events'.

The past remains contested ground, and funerals have lost none of their value as weapons to be brandished in 'the patriot game'. Dead heroes are still liable to be hi-jacked or conscripted by one side or the other; the past and its bodies are too useful to remain undisturbed. The ordinary dead Irish citizen can sleep peacefully in his or her grave, but Ireland is a cold, hard, manipulative country in handling its illustrious corpses.

Note
An earlier version of this paper was delivered at a conference in Vitoria and published as 'Cadáveres ilustres: el entierro de los héroes nacionalistas irlandeses' in *La celebración de la nación. Simbolos, mitos y lugares de memoria,* ed. Ludger Mees (Vitoria, Editorial Comares, 2012). The author wishes to acknowledge assistance from Frank Bouchier-Hayes, Maurice Bric, Marie Coleman, Anne Dolan, Bryan Fanning, Andreas Hess, Ann-Marie Kilgallon, Patrick Maume and Will Murphy.

---

[1] David Fitzpatrick, 'Commemoration in the Irish Free State: a Chronicle of Embarrassment' in *History and Memory in Modern Ireland*, ed. Ian McBride (Cambridge: Cambridge University Press, 2001), 184.
[2] Graham Greene, *Travels with my Aunt* (London, The Bodley Head, 1969), 10.
[3] Nina Witoszek, 'Ireland: a Funerary Culture?', *Studies*, 1987, 212.
[4] Shane O'Shea, *Death and Design in Victorian Glasnevin* (Dublin, Dublin Cemeteries Committee, 2000), 70.
[5] Ruth Dudley Edwards, *Sunday Independent*, 24 April 2016, 32.
[6] George Orwell, *Nineteen-Eighty-Four* (Harmondsworth: Penguin, 1954), 199.
[7] Eric Hobsbawm, *The New Century* (London: Little, Brown, 2000), 24-5; also Maurice Halbwachs, 'we appeal to our memory only in order to answer questions which others have asked us', in *On Collective Memory* (Chicago and London: University of Chicago Press, 1992), 38.

[8] *Freeman's Journal*, 20 June 1898, 6.
[9] *Freeman's Journal*, 9 August 1864, 6.
[10] *Irish Independent*, 2 October 1911, 4.
[11] *Freeman's Journal*, 3 August 1847, 3.
[12] *Freeman's Journal*, 19 September 1845, 2.
[13] Gary Owens, 'Visualizing the Liberator: Self-Fashioning, Dramaturgy, and the Construction of Daniel O'Connell', in *Éire-Ireland*, 33, 3-4, 34, 1 (1998-9), 105-16: 118.
[14] *The Nation*, 7 August 1847, 703.
[15] *Freeman's Journal*, 7 August 1847, 3.
[16] Shane O'Shea, *Death and Design*, 143-4, 153.
[17] Louis R. Bisceglia, 'The Fenian Funeral of Terence Bellew McManus', *Éire-Ireland*, 14, 3 (Fall 1979), 46-62.
[18] R. V. Comerford, *The Fenians in Context: Irish Politics and Society, 1848-82* (Dublin: Wolfhound Press, 1985), 76.
[19] Cornelia D. J. Pearsall, 'Burying the Duke: Victorian Mourning and the Funeral of the Duke of Wellington', in *Victorian Literature and Culture* (27, 2, 1999), 366.
[20] *The Irish Times*, 10 Oct. 1891, 5; 12 October 1891, 5.; Pauric Travers, '"Our Fenian Dead": Glasnevin cemetery and the genesis of the republican funeral', in *Dublin and Dubliners: Essays in the History and Literature of Dublin City*, eds James Kelly and Uáitéar MacGearailt (Dublin: Helicon, 1990), 63-4.
[21] Finerty, J.F. *Ireland in Pictures: A Grand Collection of Over 400 Magnificent Photographs of the Beauties of the Green Isle, with Historical and Descriptive Sketches.* (New York: J.S. Hyland and Co., 1898), 90.
[22] *The Irish Times*, 20 October 1891, 6.
[23] Malcolm Brown, *The Politics of Irish Literature from Thomas Davis to W. B. Yeats* (London: University of Washington Press, 1972), 211.
[24] Gary Owens, 'Nationalist Monuments in Ireland, c.1870-1914: Symbolism and Ritual' in *Ireland. Art into History*, eds Raymond Gillespie and Brian P. Kennedy (Dublin: Town House, 1994), 112-4.
[25] Thomas Laqueur, *London Review of Books*, 20 September 2001, 6.
[26] *Irish Independent*, 1 October 1917, 3-4.
[27] Thomas J. Brophy, 'Political Funerals and the Realisation of the Irish Free State, 1847-1929' (PhD dissertation, University College Dublin, 2003), 92.
[28] *Freeman's Journal*, 24 March 1875, 5.
[29] *Irish Independent*, 20 March 1907, 6.
[30] *Nationality*, 7 August 1915, 4.
[31] Patrick Maume, 'O'Donovan Rossa, Jeremiah', in *Dictionary of Irish Biography*, vol. 7, eds James McGuire and James Quinn (Dublin, Cambridge: Cambridge University Press, 2009), 425; Carla King, *The Irish Times*, 4 August 2015, 13; Shane Kenna, *Jeremiah O'Donovan Rossa: Unrepentant Fenian* (Sallins: Merrion Press, 2015), 242-4.
[32] Kathleen Clarke, *Revolutionary Woman, Kathleen Clarke, 1878-1972. An Autobiography* (Dublin, O'Brien Press, 1992), 56.
[33] Ian McBride, 'Introduction', in McBride, *History and Memory*, 31.
[34] *Irish Independent*, 1 October 1917, 4.
[35] John Lavery's *Sketch for the Funeral of Terence MacSwiney, Lord Mayor of Cork 1920* which can be found on the cover of this volume depicts the departure of MacSwiney's funeral procession from Southwark Cathedral.
[36] *Irish Independent*, 17 August 1922, 6.
[37] *Freeman's Journal*, 25 August 1922, 4
[38] *Irish Independent*, 29 August 1922, 5; 28 August 1922, 5.

[39] See Anne Dolan, *Commemorating the Irish Civil War: History and Memory, 1923-2000* (Cambridge: Cambridge University Press, 2003), 100-13.
[40] *Poblacht na h-Eireann. War news No 13*, 11 July 1922; Collins to Kitty Kiernan, ca 2 August 1922, in *In Great Haste. The Letters of Michael Collins and Kitty Kiernan*, eds León Ó Broin and Cian Ó hÉigeartaigh (Dublin: Gill and Macmillan, 1996), 219.
[41] *Freeman's Journal*, 5 August 1922, 6.
[42] *Freeman's Journal*, 31 October 1924, 6.
[43] *Irish Independent*, 14 July 1927, 7.
[44] *Irish Independent*, 18 July 1927, 8.
[45] *Dáil Eireann, Official Report*, 28, col. 1,400 (14 March 1929).
[46] Tom Garvin, 'The Discreet Charm of the National Bourgeoisie', *Third Degree*, 1, 1 (Spring 1977), 16-17.
[47] Kate Travers, 'The Tone of National Commemoration: the Annual Wolfe Tone Commemorations at Bodenstown' (MA dissertation, UCD, 2002), 35.
[48] J. G. Molloy to H. J. McCann, 21 January 1965; Lemass to Wilson, 16 February 1965; Wilson to Lemass, 19 February 1965, National Archives of Ireland, DT 96/6/190.
[49] Roisín Higgins, *Transforming 1916. Meaning, Memory and the Fiftieth Anniversary of the Easter Rising* (Cork: Cork University Press, 2012), 29.
[50] *The Irish Times*, 2 March 1965, 6.
[51] *The Irish Times*, 25 February 1965, 1; 26 February. 1965, 1.
[52] *The Irish Times*, 2 March 1965, 6.
[53] *The Irish Times*, 20 February 1976, 14; 21 February 1976, 1; 23 February 1976, 1.
[54] *The Irish Times*, 7 November 1977, 1, 6.
[55] Padraig O'Malley, *Biting at the Grave: the Irish Hunger Strikes and the Politics of Despair* (Belfast: Beacon Press, 1990), 157-8.
[56] *An Phoblacht*, 9 May 1981, 16; 30 May 1981, 23.
[57] *Ibid.*, 30 May 1981, 27.
[58] Diarmaid Ferriter, 'On the State Funerals', in *The Dublin Review*, 5 (Winter 2001-2), 9.
[59] *The Irish Times*, 30 March 2016, 6.

2 | Crying by Singing Out: Performing the Cry-die of North West Cameroon in Dublin

Sheryl Lynch

The way we think about and respond to death can reveal more about our attitudes towards, and expectations of living than any other life cycle event. The end of a life triggers a series of actions that are expected to be carried out in a codified way by the bereaved. These conventions give rise to religious, social, and creative performances that not only assist us in our mourning but also illuminate key facets of what makes us human. Anthropologists such as Boon[1] and Kan[2] agree that the mortuary ritual is an excellent place to investigate religious change, and Jindra cites it as 'a window into broader sociocultural phenomena'.[3] Musicality is a central facet of being human, and death ceremonies can be sites for immense musical ingenuity, whereby organized sound is not only a vehicle for worship and consolation but also a means to contest social norms. Music is often described by North West Cameroonians as having cathartic properties: it excites, heals and consoles. North West deaths are marked by a celebration of the deceased's life during a highly musical mortuary ritual called the cry-die. The cry-die provides a 'meaningful framework'[4] for North Westerners facing death at home and in Ireland. This chapter draws attention to the role of music in potentiating the relevance and power of the cry-die. In doing so, I shed light on the variety of responses to death present in my case study and challenge the claim that there exists a mourning style that is homogenous to West Africa.

While other scholars (e.g. Argenti and Jindra)[5] have described the cry-die as either a site for polemic expression or, in Jindra's case, in terms of Christian egalitarianism, my focus is on the utilization of the rich and varied song repertoire in constructing transnational identities. There are over 120 people from North West Cameroon currently living in Ireland. Most of the community arrived no more than twelve years ago when Ireland's economic boom attracted immigrants seeking a better future. Since 2002, the community has strengthened, set up an official organization[6] and performed at several public events (e.g. the national St Patrick's Day parade and the Festival of World Cultures). The group have fostered an indemnity ethos in their social gatherings, whereby births and deaths are celebrated as a means to perpetuate North West culture whilst providing financial and moral support to one another. Ireland's North Westerners belong to a larger cultural group known as Grassfielders but identify more strongly with the Ngemba language cluster and Mankon customs of the Bamenda area in the North West Region. Rituals that mark life and death are still performed in Ireland but are transformed in order to reflect the context of transnationalism that North Westerners find themselves in.

Encountering the Cry-die

When organising a cry-die, the *mèŋkyi mè nìwúè* (funeral dirges) are the fulcrum around which all other components function. The wealth (in both abundance and style) of funerary songs in the North West allows mourners to respond to a death within a codified and meaningful framework, regardless of the circumstances surrounding the death. The life and death of the individual is marked by the entire community at the cry-die. The crucial musicality of the event is flexible enough to provide the much needed consolation and healing for the family of the deceased and his/her community. A close consultant, Lewis Akenji, who grew up in the North West, describes the relationship of music to North West society as 'the downward slope that allows the river to flow'.[7] Music not only facilitates the survival of the society but is a central component of it, for what is a river without its bed, its meanders, and the incline which staves off stagnancy and sickness? This metaphor illuminates the indispensability of music to healthy human interaction. When applied to North West Cameroon, the metaphor signifies the importance placed upon rivers as messengers of the Divine. Rivers feature strongly in local proverbs and are viewed as the very lifeline of the North West, a symbol of the continuity of tradition and life itself. The affect of music is an essential component of North West ritual and social occasions. Lewis goes on to say that music 'opens up space for people'.[8] The cry-die provides space for the community to perform musical *responses* rather than prescriptions. Once traditional funerary songs are sung at some point in the death rite, it is deemed successful. There is no set repertoire that must be sung in a specific way that we could class as a standard or musical protocol for North West cry-dies.[9] This allows mourners to personalize death rites for each deceased individual, and respond accordingly, if, for example, a 'bad death' has taken place such as the death of a child.

During my fieldwork in Cameroon in July 2012, I attended such a cry-die. After a straight week of rain, I awoke one morning to the sound of the tall drum, a goatskin drum, usually one metre tall, ornamented with carvings of the king or *fon*, and queen *nafon*. When I heard the drum call, the blueness of a North West dawn had only begun to seep into my room at my host's house. In my sleepy state, I mistook the sound for thunder and began to resign myself to the idea that our house was going to slip down the mountain in a rush of red mud and banana trees. Instead, the reality was much worse. An eight year old boy had died of typhoid during a trip to Douala with his parents, and Akum village was now mourning his death. The palace had ordered a drum call to be sent out at dawn to inform the village that they were now in mourning. When I arrived at the house, members of the *nkwi Fon* (high ranking royal officials) were seated wearing their black hats, at the doorway of the house, wherein lay the body of the young boy. It is believed that these men have access to the spirit world and that they sit in waiting, guarding the boy and eventually bear witness to his departure from this world. The first song that was performed described how *nka* (light or spirit) had passed through the village. Subsequently, the women and neighbours began to form a circle and perform the following:

Transcription of *Ma Ka Asang* Call and Response.

Much of the melodic material can be heard to repeat over the course of a call-and-response structure, with variation for the most part restricted to the soloist's material. The lyrics here demonstrate the pervasive references to the forest found in Akum songs:

Ma Ka Asang
Translated by Juliette Chi and Nchang Divine Ndimofur

Soloist: Wo A yeah, Atu za fangne baghe le	Soloist: wo gha ye, a big tree has broken
(chorus harmonize on le)	(chorus harmonize on le)
All: Wa yeah A wo- awo- awee-ee oh	All: Wa yeah a ao a wo a wee-ee oh
S: Wo A yeah, Ge anu zee fu bangu le	S: a wo yea, that it has been so for ages
(Chorus join in on le)	(Chorus join in on le)
All: Wa yeah A wo- awo- awee-ee oh	All: Wa yeah a ao a wo a wee-ee oh
S: Wa a yeah, ma asang a ma ka le	S: Wa a yeah throw your asang

The opening few lines of this song indicate that there is a refrain, comprising mostly vocables: 'Ma ka le, way oh, Oh wo, oh wo, a we-ee, oh'. There is a strong but flexible pulse in this song, which features both duple and triple subdivisions. For example, there are triple subdivisions of duple metre during the solo call section, and duple subdivisions of duple metre during the response. For these reasons, my transcription has no bar lines. I also omit a key signature because the pitches form a pentatonic scale that hovers around 'A'. When the chorus enters at the end of the soloist's phrase, the melody is harmonized at a fourth below, in parallel motion. When reading the transcription, it is important to note that these are relative pitches. The transcription begins at the first instance of 'ma-ka-le' in the song, when the call and response initally combine to produce a fourth. An *asang* is an ornamental accoutrement made of horsehair; however, performances outside of the palace often replace the expensive *asang* with local foliage such as banana leaves. The dancers throw themselves forward with the *asang*, giving in to the grief, releasing. The higher pitch facilitates the feeling of lightness and hope. It has been noted that Akum 'death songs are marked by their solemnity and mournful tones'[10] and my field recordings would certainly support this claim. However, the event I attended was a particularly sad funeral for a small child. My main collaborator, Juliette, returned to Akum for her grandmother's funeral in the spring of 2014, and recalls a celebratory cry-die, with jovial songs in praise of the long life the woman had lived. Other cry-dies I attended in Mankon, lower Ngemba, were also far more jovial, with a song refrain of 'we are the kings of happiness' being the most popular performance of the proceedings. My conclusion is that most mortuary rites comprise mournful funeral dirges but the majority of the song repertoire is celebratory. Getting the right balance between mourning and celebration is part of the performance aesthetic of North West mortuary rituals and the variety of song styles is proof that even within a small region of Cameroon there exist vastly different styles of mourning. Ireland's Cameroonian community build on their home experience of musical responses to death while adding to this aesthetic the transformative experience of transnationalism. Before discussing cry-dies in Ireland, some background information about the North West tradition is necessary.

The North West Cry-die

Until the second half of the twentieth century, cry-die events went on for over a week but today they typically last for three days. The first day is one of mourning, a sombre day with very little music and much keening and crying. The second day is characterized by a concerted effort to celebrate the life of the deceased, play music, sing, dance, eat, and drink until the early hours of the following morning. On the third day, the bereaved participate in a purification ritual whereby heads are shaved, washed and cleansed.[11] Although these three components of a cry-die constitute what is understood as correct protocol in the event of a death, the duration and style of each ceremony differs according to such factors as the age and status of the deceased, the financial means of the family and the musical repertoire of the village native to the individual who has died.

When a member of a family dies their extended family is notified immediately. Most families have a plan (strategic and financial) that they put in motion in the event of a family death. Despite a monogamy-biased strand of Christianity taking hold of the area since the early 1950s, many polygamous marriages still existed up until the late 1970s. This has resulted in a number of very large families; one singer I know is one of 42 siblings. Family are expected to travel from abroad and participate in the rites that secure the successful passing on of their loved one's soul. The use of cell phones has transformed the way North Westerners communicate as well as transforming the expectations that those living at home place on diasporans. Francis B. Nyamnjoh explains how the ease of communication has resulted in a cessation of independence that was once afforded to North West diasporans:

> In the Bamenda Grassfields, for example, marriages, feasts, funerals, *crydie*, and village development initiatives can no longer pass by any North Westerner simply because they are

in the Diaspora. The cell phone has become like the long arm of the village leadership, capable of reaching even the most distant sons and daughters of the soil trapped in urban spaces.[12]

Ireland's North Westerners convene when a member of the community needs to travel home for a funeral. These wake keepings honour the person who has passed away back home and use the event as a means to raise the money for their friend to travel and contribute to the cry-die. The organization of a cry-die can be quite arduous when you need to gather dozens of family members from abroad. For this reason, and also for financial reasons, the celebratory aspect of the event may be postponed. It is preferable, however, to perform all three parts at the one time. Family unity is very important and the appearance of harmony and solidarity must be maintained at all costs. It is believed that the spirit of the deceased will be unhappy if the family is in a state of discord. It is well documented that the cry-die has a dual purpose of celebrating the individual whilst appeasing both the mourners *and* the deceased. In his thesis, folklorist and linguist Divine Ndimofur mentions the fear of reprisals from dissatisfied deceased.[13] He notes the categories of funeral dirges and their themes for the case of Akum; however, these categories describe funerary song content for the Grassfields in general:

Fig. 2.1) Opening dance troupe at Mankon cry-die, July 2012 (Author's photograph).

Some are particularly composed to mark the death of a beloved one. Others are composed to examine the cause or causes of the death of an individual. A number of death songs are addressed to the dead persons. One category bids farewell to the dead wishing them a safe journey back to the ancestors. Another category instructs the dead to revenge their death if it was caused by someone. Other death songs simply lament the void inconveniences and misery created by the death of a member of the family. This may be the mother or father (of the children) or the wife or husband, or simply a promising indigene of Akum.[14]

The above categories give us insights into the kind of songs that are chosen. As stated above, songs are tailored to the situation, with the family taking the role of narrators, or, if they do not wish to be the soloist, they discuss the repertoire with a particular gifted singer in the community prior to the musical performance of mourning. Family solidarity is explicitly stated as an unquestionable facet of a successful cry-die. The family sometimes pick a pattern and have a tailor make clothes for them, so that they attend all cry-die events in uniform. In addition to fortifying the appearance of unity, this makes it easier for members of the community to identify the family and avoid a ceremonial *faux pas* such as serving or seating anybody else before them.

Fig. 2.2) Soloist at cry-die, July 2012 (Author's photograph).

Although the main function of musical performance in this context is to celebrate and mourn the deceased, other salient forms of power structures and social conventions are enacted, negotiated and perpetuated. Although I'm not attempting to delineate the cry-die as a microcosm of North West social structure (at least not here), it is important to note that previously exclusive cultural genres such as masked dance, are now being transformed by musicians and dancers outside of the palatial power structure. For example, the females and youth of some North West villages continue to flout performance norms and transform masked dances to suit, reflect, and contest their social reality. Death rites are often the most conservative form of ritual in many societies and this is not surprising when one considers that funerals are organized for (predominantly and ideally) older individuals of the society. Rebellious cultural actors have not yet dared to perform their renegade masked dance at funerals, but instead participate in the secular dance troupes. Without much exception, older members of North West society hold the most conservative views. The elderly of the Grassfields are highly respected as cultural repositories, and often it is members of this section of society that are titled and have privileged access to the upper ranks of the Fon's palatial structure. When a society is compelled to face the issue of life and death head on and organize a burial for a community member, conventions about spirituality, fallibility and insecurities about one's position on and in the afterlife are put centrefold. However brave one may be about changing the routine or repertoire of ritual practice outside the domain of the mortuary cycle, it is often that deference to the norms is observed when the soul of another is believed to be at stake.

Examples of Song Repertoire

A typical funeral dirge that is sung in Cameroon and Ireland is 'We are Looking for Our Friend', performed for at least three generations but first published in Ndimofur's 2011 thesis.[15] Some key themes emerge from this song that serve as an introduction to funerary music in the North West, and how it relates to the deceased through a performance of memory. The asking of questions such as 'where did he sleep?' or 'where did she go?' reference a spatial relationship between the afterlife and 'this world', the compounds of Bafut, the banana fields of Akum, and the busy streets of Bamenda. This relationship to an unknown sacred space is central to understanding the reverence North Westerners still show to their ancestors, a reverence that emerges to the surface most clearly at birth and death rites of passage.

We are Looking for Our Friend
Translated by Nchang Divine Ndimofur

bəghə lìŋè a sun wəghə	We are looking for our friend
la a li bə ghə?	But where did he sleep?
fi ghən bəgh byir lìŋè a sun wəghə	It is late we are still looking for our friend
fi ghən bəgh byir lìŋè a sun wəghə	It is late we are still looking for our friend
abXn a ti' mi	The dance is coming to an end
bəgh byir a sun wəghə	Yet we are still looking for our friend
la a li bə ghə?	But where did he sleep?
bəghə lìŋè a sun wəghə	We are looking for our mate
nìwu tsɔ' mibì məghə a njwi tsim	Death threatens us daily
nerə tsɔ' tsɔ' la	So let it swoop down on me now
nìwu tsɔ' mibì məghə a njwi tsim	Death threatens us daily
nerə tsɔ' tsɔ' la	So let it swoop down on me now

The above song text[16] employs a common theme of looking for the deceased. When sung at cry-dies, performers seek to comfort the bereaved that may still be in the habit of looking out for their family member or friend, only to quickly realize the tragic futility of doing so. The song reaches deep into the experience of losing a loved one, and although the song is imbedded into traditional Cameroonian performance, it resonates universally for anyone who has lost a close friend or relative. The words '*abXn a ti' mi*' (the dance is coming to an end) relate to an omnipresent North West narrative: that of life as a performance. During my fieldwork in Akum, the human life cycle was referred to as a song, a dance and, once, a journey, with the women who came to talk to my host (Ma U) and myself each evening after dark. Perhaps this was because they knew I came to study the music of the area and how it relates to the community, but I somehow doubt it. Indeed, over the years, my key consultant and frequent singer, Juliette, has referred to music itself as life or a vital source of support on many occasions during our conversations at her kitchen table in Crumlin, a southern suburb of Dublin. The song also introduces us to a discourse of defiance and bravery in the face of death with the words:

nìwu tsɔ' mibì məghə a njwi tsim	Death threatens us daily
nerə tsɔ' tsɔ' la	So let it swoop down on me now

The acceptance of death is clearly illustrated in the song from the Akum cry-die: *Ge anu zee fu bangu le*. The meaning of *Ge anu zee fu bangu le* as told to me by Juliette Chi is 'death has happened since the beginning of time, it is not to upset you today'. This acceptance of our life cycle is tantamount to the bereavement process and the normalization of the occurrence of death is sung out in an effort to mitigate the element of shock that mourners invariably feel despite the inevitability of death. The defiant 'So let it swoop down on me now' in 'We are Looking for Our Friend' is a particularly overt example of demonstrating bravery. Such acts are important displays of strength which dramatize the fears of the community and subsequently quell them by continuing to sing, participate and generally illustrate aliveness and continuity alongside an event that is unequivocally focused on the cessation of life. The sung performance of defiance and the irreverence shown to death by these lyrics cultivates a sense of stability, strength and solidarity necessary for all to contribute to not just this communal event, but to the survival of the community in general.

A Performance of Remembering – Cry-dies in Ireland

Having pointed to some ritual functions of cry-dies in Cameroonian spiritual and social life, I now turn my attention to the cry-die in the diasporic context. The terms used for mortuary rituals in Ireland vary. Often they are referred to as cry-dies and sometimes as wake keeping, indicative of the Christian ritual format many North Westerners engage with here. The processes and projects of remembering remain consistent despite this engendered lexical difference, a difference which may point to distinct processes of transformation in the future. North West performances of repertoire from a previous home, in a diasporic context, function to commemorate not only the deceased but also a previous way of being, a previous engagement with social memory. Music functions as a medium for remembering and, in line with Mitchell's definition of a medium, music may be understood as:

> A complex social institution that contains individuals within it, and is constituted by a *history of practices*, rituals and habits, skills and techniques, as well as by a set of material objects and spaces.[17]

The 'history of practices' pertaining to North West mortuary rituals is in a constant state of renegotiation. For example, the privilege of a cry-die has only been extended to non-royals since the early twentieth century, a consequence of Christian egalitarian attitudes to the afterlife. For this reason, Paul Connerton's 'inscribing' versus 'incorporating' practices are relevant distinguishers in the interpretation of performing memory at cry-dies.[18] The three ritual components of death rites such as the wake keeping (mourning), burial, and celebratory cry-die are inscribed, transmitted as a meme, conventionalized; however, the interpretative, personalized musical performances are part of the incorporated memory of the region: dances and songs are transmitted and transformed from body to body, from Cameroon to Ireland, and transformed to adapt to the circumstance within the ritual framework. In this way, I concur with Plate and Smelik's[19] recent interpretation of Connerton's bifurcated theory of memory as functioning on a continuum. North West performances are not acts of presentism, nor re-enactments of static convention. Rather, they are functional, cultural acts that exemplify the cross-temporality (see Schneider)[20] evident in every other area of their life where the past and present continually inform each other. Operating on this continuum, there are two salient ways of remembering during the Irish cry-die, which I have interpreted in terms of their function.

Performing (for) the Present	**Performing (commemorating) the Past**
Function	Function
(a) Enacts a North West identity in Ireland	(a) Commemorates the deceased
(b) Consoles Family and Friends	(b) Embodies a 'history of practices' (Mitchell)[21]

These functions were illustrated clearly at a cry-die in Clondalkin Towers Accommodation Centre (a refugee centre) on 21 June 2013. Some North Westerners live in temporary accommodation such as this, others own their own homes, and others rent apartments or houses in urban centres of Dublin and Cork and commuter towns such as Drogheda. The common place of origin unites North Westerners in Ireland despite differences in early migrant employment and accommodation circumstances. Remembering becomes a critical project for displaced and newly placed people, occupying an uncertain space in a new home. Members of the community attend wakes of people unknown to them to comfort each other and to appear to themselves as themselves. Juliette Chi, a soloist at many North West events, speaks of music as being

> like hope, when you are singing, it's like hope. It's like unity and hope at the same time and coming together, *making something to still be together*. Music is life, music is love. Music is everything![22]

Performing songs from the North West is crucial as '[m]usic is in many migrant contexts a particularly important means of making a home, and imagining a future'.[23] Life cycle events are transformed in the migrant context and given a dual role: commemoration *and* the maintenance of solidarity. The cry-die was for a grandmother who lived and died in North West Cameroon; her daughter has lived in Ireland for 12 years. The daughter is of North West origin and her husband is from the South East, Francophone region. This was my first 'mixed' event, as North Westerners usually host their own events, often consciously differentiating themselves from Francophone Cameroonians. The live performance was provided by the Women of Substance group, an all-female North West association. The call and response singing and dancing in a circle to the rhythm of the songs such as 'We are Looking for Our Friend' was preserved from a tradition particular to the North West. Performing (for) the Present was evidenced in the way the musical performance enacted a North West identity in Ireland and sought to console family and friends.

'They cry by singing out'[24]

The responsibility to provide live music at the cry-die was given to the women of the North West community, who are widely referred to as a people who 'love their indigenous music heritage', and have not been as 'successful in producing local pop stars'.[25] Of course, this view is not shared by all North Westerners; however, it is important to note that an environment of cultural propaganda is something that has informed musical practice at home, and is not solely a product of migrancy. The Women of Substance group walked purposefully to the centre of the room to perform their songs at the wake keeping and give their sister a North West send off. The attitudes expressed by the North Westerners were of pride in their cultural knowledge. The wake became a site for remembering the present migrant reality of the North Westerners in Ireland; a site for the embodiment of that identity. The fact that this performance was enacted in front of their Francophone neighbours afforded them extra satisfaction in light of the tension between the Anglophone and Francophone regions, the North West separatist biography, and the long cultural opposition to centralization from a largely ostracized North West Region (see Piet Konings and Francis B. Nyamnjoh for more information).[26] Singing in Cameroonian Pidgin English and North West dialects such as Akum played out an identity specific to the North West. This identity was performed to one another; it functioned as a performance to the present context of North Westerners in Ireland. Another key function of this performance for the present is its cathartic property, as evidenced by the following song:

Tie Your Heart
Translated by Juliette Chi and Nchang Divine Ndimofur

Na so the world i dey	Such is the world
Your mama go die leave you	Your mother will die leaving you
Na so the world i dey	Such is the world
Your papa go die leave	Your father will die leaving you
Sister tie your heart of	Sister take heart
Soloist: Na so the World	Soloist: Such is the world
All: Na so the world i dey	All: Such is the world
Soloist: Your mama go die leave you	Soloist: Your mother will die leaving you
All: Na so the world i dey	All: Such is the world
Soloist: Your papa go die leave you	Soloist: Your father will die leaving you
All: Na so the world i dey	All: Such is the world

'Tie your Heart' means to 'take heart' or, more accurately, 'soften your heart'. The North West Women's group sing this for all who are physically present in that room in Clondalkin, and for the family back home in Cameroon. The soloist of the evening, Juliette Chi, describes the mourners as 'crying by singing out'.[27] It is through the performative act of song that the mourning conventions are abided. It is also implied that the style of singing and the repertory are to be 'from home'; i.e. in order to cry by singing out, you must do so within the framework of the North West cry-die.

The migrant context has meant that mortuary rites are now performed in multiple sites, with certain components only possible in the home country, for example, Juju masked dance and the burial are still preferably carried out on Cameroonian soil. The wake keeping in Ireland was consistent with the instantiation of Christian tropes within the cry-die framework, as exemplified by a song called 'The Lord say Whom Shall I Send?' This song offers consolation in stating the direct link between God's will and its effect on his followers. The willingness to 'go' and its normalization is sung out to expel the fear of the afterlife. Singing this song in English echoes the teachings of Anglophone Irish Catholic nuns present in North West education institutions since the beginning of missionary schools in the early twentieth century. The presence of these Irish educators has undoubtedly contributed to the strong sense of belonging that many North Westerners feel in Ireland. 'The Lord say Whom Shall I Send?' is then performed in Bagangu (Akum); the Akum dialect identifying the text as exclusively North West, a musical offering from one North Westerner to another.

The second style of remembering I wish to focus on is Performing (commemorating) the Past, serving to commemorate the deceased and embody a 'history of practices'. The wake keeping performs the past as it recollects the memory of the deceased by upholding her image for the entire evening. I recall a vivid image of her photograph in an ornate frame bobbing up and down amongst living dancing bodies, her image swaying back and forth, animated by the present (Fig. 2.3).

Fig. 2.3) Photograph of deceased held up by granddaughter at Clondalkin cry-die (Author's photograph, 21 June 2013).

The utilization of the photograph is to commemorate the past by positioning the figure of the deceased in front of the eyes of the living and among the moving bodies of the present. The family that has lost the person addresses the people who have come to the wake, recalling their favourite memories of the deceased. Songs are personalized for the particular person who has passed away, changing the third person pronoun accordingly. For example, the family that has lost the person addresses the people who have come to the wake, recalling their favourite memories of the deceased. Personalization and the singing-in of migrancy are evident in improvized song lyrics such as the following:

You pray for me and I pray for you
Translated by Juliette Chi

Soloist: The road is slippy but she won't turn back
Why don't you pray for her?
Oh sisters, Oh brothers, Oh Children
 (Cameroonian Pidgin English: picking [pIkIn])
In Ireland, you pray for me and I pray for you

This song is continually transformed for the particular person who has passed away, changing the third person pronoun accordingly. It is also personalized in terms of who the song is attempting to console e.g fellow migrants, sisters, brothers, parents or children.

Conclusion: Crying in Context, Singing Together

The Irish cry-die enacts a *history of practices* by maintaining linguistic practices, themes and proverbs from the North West in their mourning songs. The gatherings in Ireland are participatory spaces whereby the community use musical performance as a means to support one another financially and emotionally; however, each event differs in character and cannot be justifiably described in contrast to 'Western funerals', which are themselves diverse and dynamic rituals.[28] Ingrid Monson criticises Charles Keil (2005) and John Miller Chernoff (1979) for over-emphasizing and idealizing the 'participatory, egalitarian, and spiritual qualities of African diasporic musics', resulting in the neglect of areas such as 'intracultural power stratifications and processes of contestation.'[29] Scholars are more tentative when it comes to deconstructing long-held beliefs about communalism in *West* African musics and, crucially, pan-West Africanism in general. The Grassfields constitute one fifth of Cameroon's total population, and although there are many shared cultural characteristics, enough in fact to warrant the term pan-North West style, the examples I have presented here are proof of the cultural complexity evident in the musical traditions in one part of Cameroon. The examples challenge the idea that there is a 'West African funeral' and illustrate that the rituals performed when a death occurs are flexible and musically responsive to the context.

To conclude, I wish to reiterate that cry-dies 'work' in the Grassfields because the highly respected older traditional beliefs are 'given space' (to echo my consultant Lewis here) in the ritual, while newer forms of social performance are also enacted. The ritual is seen as a success if the three components are upheld; however, the musical catharsis (the crying by singing out) is ensured only if performers are responsive to the circumstances surrounding the death. This is more complex than merely whipping out a catalogue of sad songs if 'bad' death occurs; rather, songs must include proverbs from the village of the deceased chosen by the core members of their family, and either permit or omit Juju dancers and percussive instrumentation. The cry-die is a site where newly instantiated tropes of Christianity and capitalism have been assimilated into traditional beliefs about the power of sound. The cry-die functions as a meaningful framework for North Westerners because a) it is a respected and indispensable space for performing memory and b) the framework is flexible enough *musically* – although definitely not structurally – in order to serve as a cathartic tool for the community. Music from back home re-emerges in the Irish context as the community do the work of remembering through projects of performing the past for the present. The cry-die illustrates that music can tell us a lot about what a community remembers, how they remember each other, and what they refuse to forget.

---

[1] James Boon, 'Anthropology, Ethnology, and Religion', in *Encyclopaedia of Religion,* ed. Mircea Eliade (New York: MacMillan, 1987), 315.

[2] Sergei Kan, 'Anthropology of Death in the Late 1980s', in *Reviews of Anthropology*, 20 (1992), 283-300: 299. See also Richard Huntington and Peter Metcalf, *Celebrations of Death: The Anthropology of Mortuary Ritual,* Second Edition (Cambridge: Cambridge University Press, 1991).

[3] Michael Jindra, 'Christianity and the Proliferation of Ancestors: Changes in Hierarchy and Mortuary Ritual in the Cameroon Grassfields', in *Africa: Journal of the International African Institute*, 75/3 (London: Cambridge University Press, 2005), 356-77: 357.

[4] Clifford Geertz, 'Ritual and Social Change, a Javanese Example', in *The Interpretation of Cultures* (New York: Basic Books, 1973), 142-69: 164.

[5] Nicholas Argenti, 'Dancing in the Borderlands: the Forbidden Masquerades of Oku Youth and Women (Cameroon)', in *Makers and Breakers: Children and Youth in Postcolonial Africa,* eds de Boeck, F. and Honwana, A. (Oxford, UK : James Currey Publishers), 121-49, and Jindra ,'Christianity and the Proliferation of Ancestors: Changes in Hierarchy and Mortuary Ritual in the Cameroon Grassfields'.

[6] www.nowacire.com, accessed 22 February 2015.

[7] Interview with Lewis Akenji, 14 September 2012.

[8] Interview with Lewis Akenji, 14 September 2012.

[9] This is my observation and is also noted by a number of my collaborators, and by Ndimofur, *Oral Literature of the Akum People: A Case Study of the Folksong and Cultural Elements* (Unpublished Thesis, 2011), 32.

[10] *Ibid*, 40.

[11] Jindra, 'Christianity and the Proliferation of Ancestors', 359.

[12] Francis B. Nyamnjoh, *Africa's Media: Democracy and the Politics of Belonging*, (London: ZED Press, 2005), also cited in Walter Gam Nkwi, *Voicing the Voiceless*, 120.

[13] Divine Ndimofur, *Oral Literature of the Akum People*, 32.

[14] *Ibid.*

[15] *Ibid.*

[16] The text of this song is set in the International Phonetic Alphabet.

[17] W.J.T. Mitchell, *What do Pictures Want? The Lives and Loves of Images* (Chicago: University of Chicago Press, 2005), 213.

[18] Paul Connerton, *How Societies Remember* (Cambridge: Cambridge University Press, 1989), 73.

[19] *Performing Memory in Art and Popular Culture,* eds Liedeke Plate and Anneke Smelik (Routledge, New York, 2013), 4.
[20] Rebecca Schneider, *Performing Remains: Art and War in Times of Theatrical Reenactment* (New York: Routledge, 2011), 149.
[21] W.J.T. Mitchell, *What do Pictures Want? The Lives and Loves of Images* (Chicago: University of Chicago Press, 2005), 213.
[22] Interview with Juliette Chi, 3 April 2009, emphasis mine.
[23] Martin Stokes, 'Migrant/migrating music in the Mediterranean', in *Migrating Music,* eds Jason Toynbee and Byron Dueck (London: Routledge, 2011), 28-77: 31.
[24] Interview with Juliette Chi, 1 April 2013.
[25] Francis B. Nyamnjoh and Jude Fokwang, 'Entertaining Repression: Music and Politics in Postcolonial Cameroon', in *African Affairs* 104/415 (2005), 261.
[26] Piet Konings and Francis B. Nyamnjoh, 1997, 'The Anglophone Problem', in *The Journal of Modern African Studies* 35/2 (June, 1997), 207-229.
[27] Interview with Juliette Chi: 1 April 2013.
[28] Philip Tagg, 'Universal Music and the Case of Death', in *Critical Quarterly*, 35 (1993), 54-85. Article first published online: 28 September, 2007: DOI: 10.1111/j.1467-8705.1993.tb00469.x, accessed 25 August 2014.
[29] Ingrid Monson, 'Introduction', in *The African Diaspora: a Musical Perspective* (New York: Routledge, 2003), 2.

3 | The Tomb of Pietro da Cortona in Santi Luca e Martina al Foro

Corinna Ricasoli

The renowned painter, sculptor and architect Pietro Berrettini da Cortona (1596-1669) may be considered as one of the greatest exponents of a flamboyant Roman baroque style. He reached the peak of his artistic and professional development during the 1630s – the decade that encompassed the completion of his extraordinary frescoed ceiling for the grand salon of the Palazzo Barberini (1632-1639) and his tenure, from 1634 to 1636, as president, or *principe*, of the Roman painters' organization, the Accademia di San Luca. During these years, he also began the reconstruction of the Roman Church of Santi Luca e Martina al Foro (Fig. 3.1), in which he was eventually buried. The building was, and still is, the church of the Accademia di San Luca, and the monument to Pietro da Cortona, housed within it, is an excellent example of the

Fig. 3.1) Pietro da Cortona, façade of the Church of Santi Luca e Martina al Foro, *c.* 1669.

vicissitudes of tomb building in baroque Rome and the period's new appetite for grandiose memorials to painters, sculptors and architects. At the same time, the narrative of its development highlights how such projects could be still born, or frustrated, not just by external factors but also by the professional jealousy of artists themselves.

The way in which seventeenth-century Roman artists developed a growing preoccupation with their posthumous reputations and the need for public memorials to their greatness is a phenomenon that has received insufficient attention. Pietro's monument is a particularly interesting case study, but in order to fully appreciate its significance, one must also address the controversies which surrounded the artist's involvement in the remodelling of Santi Luca e Martina al Foro as a whole – arguably, the church itself may be considered to be Pietro's real monument. That Pietro also regarded it as such, and that some of his rivals were indignant at this presumption is certainly worthy of greater discussion. Strangely, with regard to the extensive literature on Pietro da Cortona, scholars have mainly limited themselves to delineating the historical events and archival documents related to the construction of the church and to Pietro's memorial. This essay attempts to address this critical lacuna, by offering a far more analytical commentary as a means of illuminating the personal and political ambitions enmeshed in the artist's efforts to secure the grandiose reconstruction of the church of the Accademia di San Luca. This will also reveal how it was not just Pietro's own burial and memorialization that had agency in this process: his conveniently dramatic discovery and re-interment of the bodies of four early Christian martyrs also reveals how the grand architectural projects of the Roman Counter-Reformation also drew their life from shrines to the long dead.

A Temple to the Patron Saint of Artists: St Luke's Church

The first seat of the Roman painters' guild was at the Church of San Luca, located on the slope of the Esquiline Hill, near the Basilica of Santa Maria Maggiore. Toward the end of the 16th century, Pope Sixtus V Peretti (1520-1590, r.1585-1590) decided to make improvements to the urban fabric of this area, and a series of demolitions took place which swept away the Church of San Luca. In recompense, in 1588, Sixtus gave the painters of Rome the Church of Santa Martina at the Forum ('al Foro'). It was jointly rededicated to Santa Martina and San Luca (St Luke being the traditional patron saint of painters and artists generally), and it became known as San Luca in Santa Martina (now Santi Luca e Martina al Foro).[1] The church was a modest, rather decrepit, single-naved structure, and by the end of the century the guild, which had now become an Academy, drew up proposals for its ambitious reconstruction. The aim was clear: the new building had to be worthy not only of the evangelist patron of the arts, but also a highly visual emblem of Rome's burgeoning and revitalized academy of painters.[2] The organization was now benefitting from a much-longed-for improvement in the social and intellectual status of the artist, which characterized later Italian renaissance culture.

In the years 1593-1594, the incumbent *principe* of the Accademia di San Luca was the late Mannerist painter Federico Zuccari (c.1541-1609). He was an artist of an intellectual frame of mind, ambitious for the Academy and all it stood for, and he spearheaded proposals for the reconstruction of its academic church. However, at this point the Accademia di San Luca's plans for the church came to nothing because the hoped-for financial support of both the Pope and the Accademia's Cardinal Protector Federico Borromeo (1564-1631) failed to materialize.[3] Therefore, the painters had to limit themselves to minor interventions to the fabric as a means of merely arresting further dilapidation.[4] After Federico Zuccari's death, the Accademia continually lacked the support of an important and influential patron – one powerful enough to ensure the necessarily formidable funds to subsidize a proper reconstruction of the church.[5] However, hope was rekindled with the election of Maffeo Barberini as Pope Urban VIII in 1623 (1568-1644, r.1623-1644) – the Barberini family had long been protectors and supporters of a number of artists including Pietro da Cortona, Gianlorenzo Bernini (1598-1680), and the painter Simon Vouet (1590-1649). It must have seemed especially fortuitous that the latter was serving as *principe* of the Accademia when the Pope's wealthy and cultured nephew Francesco Barberini (1597-1679) was appointed as Cardinal Protector of the Accademia in 1627.[6] However, in that same year the office of *principe* passed to Ottavio Leoni (1578-1630), a colleague who was not as closely allied to the Barberini, and progress towards a full reconstruction of the church stalled completely.[7] By this point, Pietro da Cortona had become the galvanizing force behind plans for reconstruction but another obstacle presented itself in the form of a fellow academician – no less a figure than Rome's premier artist: Gianlorenzo Bernini. Karl Noehles has speculated that Bernini – either out of fear or envy, or both – may have consistently frustrated those artists who, like himself, enjoyed the benefits of Barberini patronage.[8] Despite such obstacles, in 1628, Pietro's efforts still earned him an, albeit unsuccessful, candidacy for the office of *principe*, and he was perhaps helped in this thanks to the sponsorship of the influential scholar, patron and antiquarian Cassiano dal Pozzo (1588-1657). But it was Ottavio Leoni who won a second tour of duty, and he was succeeded by series of artists who failed to advance Pietro's ambitions for the church. In order, these *principi* included Baldassarre Croce (†1628), Giuseppe Cesari (also known as the Cavalier d'Arpino, †1640), Bernini, Giovanni Lanfranco (†1647), and Francesco Mochi (†1654), whose tenure ended in 1634.[9] Bernini's possible wish to frustrate Pietro has already been mentioned, but it is odd that none of the others championed the reconstruction of Santa Martina, or took the project to heart.[10] Perhaps, they had no interest in promoting such an ambitious project, as they recognized the enormous scale of the task in terms of both patronage and design.

A Shrine for the Martyrs: Santa Martina's Church

Pietro was finally elected *principe* of the Accademia di San Luca in 1634, when he was engaged upon his aforementioned masterpiece in painting, the frescoed ceiling of the grand salon of the Palazzo Barberini. To all intents and purposes, he was now court painter to the Barberini and a wealthy figure of great influence in the Roman art world.[11] This meant that, from the very first meeting under his tenure as *principe* of the Accademia, the issue of the Accademia's church took on primary importance.[12] Not without difficulty, Pietro convinced his fellow academicians to finance some pressing structural interventions at the very least.[13] However, it was at his own expense that Pietro undertook the preliminary renovation of the building's crypt, or Confessio, in order to reinforce the structure's insecure foundations. But he also had another mission in mind. This involved a quest for the relics of the church's original titular saint, the venerable late antique martyr St Martina. According to tradition, she was buried in the church in an unidentified place.[14] It is of course misleading to think of this adventure merely in terms of either personal piety, which in Pietro's case was genuine and considerable, or a precocious interest in archaeology. Pietro surely knew what he was about, and would have been well aware of the conditions conducive to grandiose church-building projects in Counter-Reformation Rome; these could not be guaranteed solely by an appreciation of the arts, or even respect for the Accademia di San Luca. The discovery of the relics of Santa Martina would be an event of such significance that it would surely arouse the spiritual fervour of Rome's populace, igniting interest in her church and sepulchre. More crucially, it would also galvanize support for Pietro's plans on the part of Cardinal Francesco Barberini and the Pope himself. Pietro possibly recalled how, following the discovery of the remains of St Bibiana ten years earlier, Pope Urban VIII and Cardinal Francesco were impelled to fund the expensive rebuilding and redecoration of that saint's titular church in the Rione Esquilino.[15] In October 1634, during an excavation near the ancient altar in the crypt of Santa Martina (where Pietro was also now planning to build his own memorial tomb – see below), the artist-turned-relic-hunter conveniently hit the jackpot: not only had he succeeded in unearthing the supposed remains of St Martina, he also stumbled upon the bodies of three other martyr saints (Epifanio, Concordio and 'a friend of theirs' whose name is unknown) into the bargain.[16] The popular fuss that greeted this miraculous discovery was satisfyingly enormous. In fact, multiple processions were organized and, in the wake of all the excitement, Pietro's confessor, the Oratorian priest Marsilio Honorati (1577-1654) was moved to write a detailed chronicle of the discovery.[17]

The incident confirms the generative power of the bodies of long dead saints in Baroque Rome, and Pietro seized the opportunity to make the first generous donation (500 scudi) for the embellishment of the lower church. His example was then followed by a series of wealthy noblemen and clerics including – finally – Cardinal Francesco Barberini, and Pope Urban VIII himself. The latter two were now acting as the upper church's main sponsors, and the programme of reconstruction was wholly entrusted to Pietro without any further discussion.[18] Work started shortly after the discovery of the relics which, in 1635, were re-interred below the main altar of the crypt, underneath the area in which, at some point during the previous year, the Accademia had informally given Pietro permission to build his own tomb.[19] This was granted before the unearthing of the relics, and on condition that he would pay for the renovation of the whole area. The game-changing discovery of the relics meant that the crypt could no longer become merely Pietro's place of burial. The *Confessio* had now taken on a new significance within the church's spatial / spiritual hierarchy and would primarily function as the memorial Chapel of St Martina and the other saints buried with her.[20] However, even as Pietro's tenure as *principe* came to an end in 1636, he refused to relinquish his claim to jus patronatus of the lower church, and retained the option of having himself buried and memorialized here. This continually rankled with other members of the Accademia di San Luca and was the cause of a dispute which would rumble on for decades, and which finally came to a head in the years following Pietro's death in 1669 (see below).

As well as restoring the lower church at his own expense, Pietro da Cortona now modified his plans so that the whole crypt would have an architectural context better suited to an area of worship (Figs. 3.2-3.4), and this would also ensure that an altar could be built above the saints' solemn place of burial (Figs. 3.5-3.6).[21] Construction began in 1641, and progressed rather slowly throughout 1642 and into 1643. Pietro's nephew, the sculptor Luca Berrettini (1609-1680), supervized the work in these years because, in 1640, Pietro himself was forced to quit Rome for Florence at the behest of Cardinal Giulio Cesare Sacchetti (1586-1663).[22] Pietro then entered the service of the Grand Duke of Tuscany Ferdinando II de' Medici (1610-1670, r.1621-1670), who commissioned him to fresco the Camera della Stufa in the Palazzo Pitti, along with other rooms in the same building.[23] Pietro's Florentine sojourn obviously did not assist progress in the lower and upper church of Santi Luca e Martina, which then suffered a series of slowdowns and setbacks.[24] The situation worsened with the death of the Barberini Pope Urban VIII. As for the new pontiff – Giovanni Battista Pamphilj, elected as Innocent X (1574-1655, r.1644-1655) – both he and his family were enemies of the Barberini.[25] As soon as he was ordained, Innocent X began a series of investigations into how and why the assets of the Barberini family had greatly increased during Urban VIII's papacy.[26] After a few months, in order to escape from charges relating to the misappropriation of funds and similar matters, the Barberini fled to France, and received the protection of Cardinal Mazarin (1602-1661).[27] Despite this turn of events, Pietro still hoped to finish the *Confessio* (at his own expense), if only for the personal satisfaction of seeing his work completed.[28]

However, in 1648 the situation changed again. Francesco Barberini returned to Rome as an emissary of Cardinal Mazarin, and over the next five years the Pamphilj and the Barberini were gradually reconciled.[29] Cardinal Barberini was able to resume his funding of construction at the church of the Accademia di San Luca; in fact, work in the upper church resumed at full speed from 1650.[30] Pietro also wanted to make further improvements to the lower church in order to provide it with greater natural light, but was not able to start work immediately. This is because he was financially stretched on several fronts, and had become involved with other projects, including the construction of a lavish silver frontal for the altar of St Margaret in the basilica dedicated to her in his hometown of Cortona, which was paid for out of his own pocket. Even at Santi Luca e Martina he had diverted his energies into a subsidiary project that involved the construction and adornment of the Chapel of St Lazarus in the upper church (Fig. 3.7), of which he was also the sponsor.[31]

The Chapel of St Lazarus further reflects how the role Pietro da Cortona assumed in the splendid refurbishment of the Church of Santi Luca e Martina increased progressively, as he began to personally supervize the reconstruction of the whole church.[32] He went about this

Fig. 3.2) View of the crypt or *Confessio*.

Fig. 3.3) View of the crypt or *Confessio*.

Fig. 3.4) View of the crypt or *Confessio*.

Fig. 3.5) View from behind of the bronze altar in the *Confessio*, designed by Pietro da Cortona, marking the burial site of St Martina and the other martyrs.

Fig. 3.6) Front view of the bronze altar in the *Confessio*, designed by Pietro da Cortona, marking the burial site of St Martina and the other martyrs.

task with extreme care and, whenever possible, he closely supervized every aspect of construction and decoration.[33] However, Cardinal Barberini's financial support eventually began to diminish, and the bountiful funds that Pietro relied upon during the 1630s gradually decreased to only 50 scudi a month. As a result, often Pietro had to pay unforeseen expenses out of his own, not limitless pockets.[34] However, between 1657 and 1661, Pietro was able to carry out the improvements planned for the lower church, as well as other decorative work.[35] As far as the upper church was concerned, the dome and the lantern (Fig. 3.8) were finished in 1664.

Academic Politics and Envy: Pietro's Church

Pietro da Cortona died on 16 May 1669 and his funeral took place in Santi Luca e Martina – the church that had now become a monument to his own tireless enterprise. By this point, the building – a single-nave greek-cross church (Fig. 3.9) – was substantially complete: only small interventions were needed in the interior, whereas the façade was (and remains) unfinished.[36] The scholar and collector Lione Pascoli (1674-1744) recounts that Pietro left 'a fund of one hundred and more thousand scudi to the church of Santa Martina' and that he reaffirmed his intentions

Fig. 3.7) View of the Chapel of St Lazarus.

to be buried there. Many people attended Pietro's funeral, more than a hundred members of the Accademia di San Luca among them. Also present were members of the Congregazione dei Virtuosi al Pantheon, and the Deputies of the Congregazione di Santa Eufemia, to whom Pietro entrusted the administration of his property (see below).[37]

As early as 1636, in the first will drawn up by Pietro da Cortona, the artist had asked to be buried in the crypt or *Confessio* of the church. As previously highlighted, this was in accordance with permission unofficially granted to him by the Accademia di San Luca sometime before.[38] However, plans for his place of burial were necessarily subject to change as Pietro's discovery of the relics of Santa Martina and her companions reoriented and elevated the function of this area of the lower church. Although Pietro still – perhaps as a point of principle – petitioned

Fig. 3.8) View of the dome and lantern.

for rights of burial in the *Confessio*, it is very likely that he then began to plan that his interment should actually take place in the Chapel of St Lazarus, of which he held the patronage, in the upper church. A drawing in the Royal Library at Windsor Castle (Inv.904449), perhaps dateable to the 1650s, shows a monument to the artist which was probably designed specifically for the chapel in question, given the monument's relatively small dimensions. The drawing is currently inventoried as by Pietro da Cortona himself, but only on stylistic grounds. Noehles and Merz convincingly consider it to be by the hand of Ciro Ferri (1634-1689) – Pietro's main student and the artist destined to continue his master's work in the church. The drawing represents a wall-memorial tomb consisting of a niche framed by garlands.[39] Within this, there is the bust of Pietro above a simple-enough sarcophagus, supported by a pedestal bearing an illegible inscription. This is clearly a study for a possible funerary monument, but certainly not a final and definitive project despite the fact that the drawing itself is highly finished. The phytomorphic decorations at the sides of the niche are divergent with one another, as are the decorations of the capitals, which are not placed symmetrically on the monument. Moreover, the volutes formed by acanthus leaves below the bust also differ. Therefore, the drawing seems intended to demonstrate a variety of decorative solutions. In all probability, this design was conceived as a 'tribute' to Pietro da Cortona, on the part of Ciro Ferri, or another one of his students. Whether it was conceived with Pietro's knowledge and blessing is a moot point: Pietro

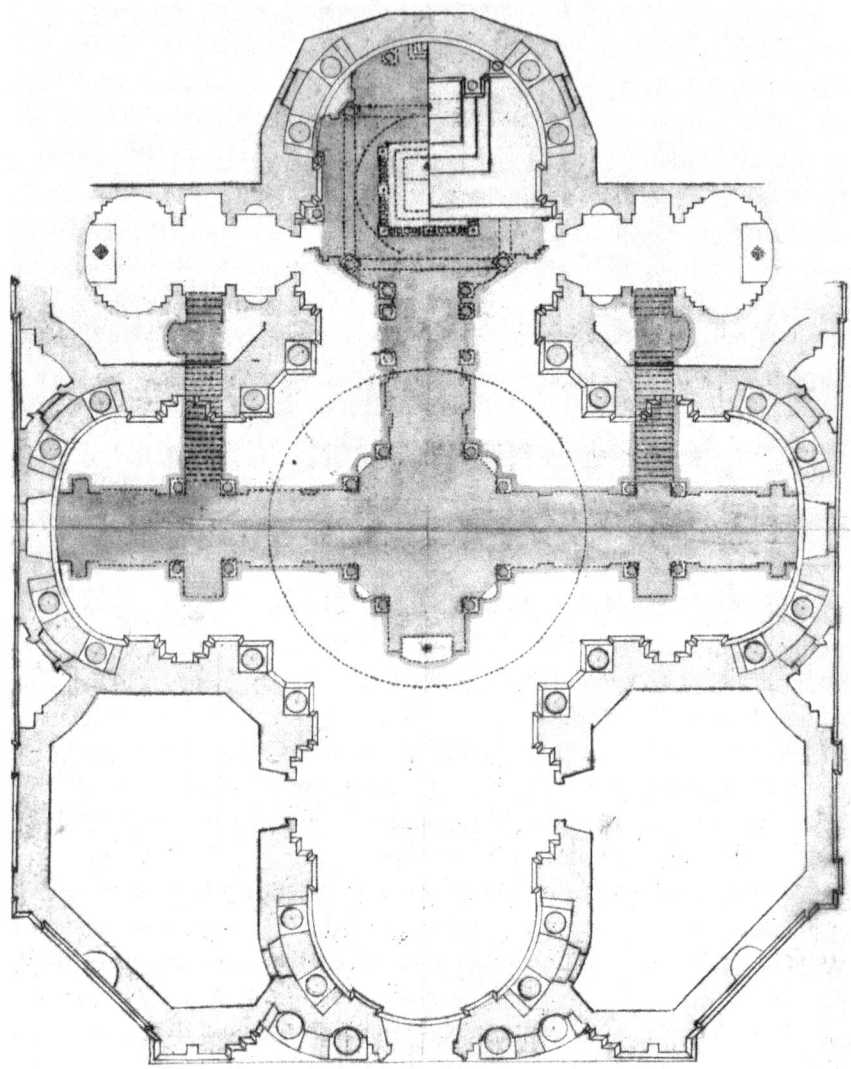

Fig. 3.9) Domenico Martinelli, Plan of the upper and lower Church. Pencil, brown ink, pen, wash, 536 x 416 mm. Milan, Civico Gabinetto dei Disegni, Castello Sforzesco, inv. SM_1,3. The darker area, shaped like an upside-down T, is the lower church, or *Confessio*. Copyright Comune di Milano – all rights reserved.

had certainly diverted a great deal of his energy into the remodelling of this personally-sponsored chapel, and it is logical that it should have been located here. That the design dates from a point at which Pietro was still hale and hearty is suggested by the fact that he personally seems to have specified exactly where he was to be buried only as his life was finally drawing to a close. Indeed, a few days before his death, Pietro drew up his second, last and longer will, in which he again asked to be buried in the Church of Santi Luca e Martina, but neither in the *Confessio* (which was now barred to him) or in the Chapel of St Lazarus. Instead, he now wished to be buried near the front door, 'and should a gravestone or another ornament be placed on my burial, I want it to be simple and that it may serve as part of the floor'.[40] The factors underlying Pietro's change of mind provide plenty of food for thought: although he asked for the gravestone to be simple and serve as part of the floor, he did not specify an inscription. But then, neither did he suggest that he should be buried anonymously, and it is interesting to note that the present grave, which is indeed marked by a large marble slab bearing an inscription (Fig. 3.10), is one of the first things that the visitor encounters on entering the church (Fig. 3.11) – suggesting an immediate and unabashed connection between the building and its architect. At the same time, the absence of a noticeable tomb also suggests that the whole church could stand as Pietro's own monument. In other words, the lack of a monumental grave to the famous 'builder of the church' creates a void which only the church itself can fill.

Fig. 3.10) Tomb of Pietro da Cortona, 1669.

Let us turn back to Pietro's last will: in addition to his burial indications, the lower church of Santa Martina was named as beneficiary of his princely capital.[41] The tombstone, sponsored by Cardinal Barberini (oddly, Pietro did not set aside a sum of money for his tomb in his will), is still *in loco* and its inscription (Fig. 3.10) reads:

> TO GOD MOST GOOD, MOST GREAT. / TO THE CAVALIER PIETRO BERRETTINI, NOBLEMAN / FROM CORTONA, FAMOUS IN THE FINE ARTS, / PAINTING AND ARCHITECTURE, / DEAR TO PRINCES, KINGS AND POPES / FOR HIS GREAT SKILL IN THE ARTS / AND THE PROBITY OF HIS MORALS; / GREATLY DEVOTED TO SANTA MARTINA, / IN ORDER TO PRESERVE [HER] SACRED ASHES / HE BUILT WITH GREAT MUNIFICENCE, / AT HIS EXPENSE, THE TOMB AND HE BEQUEATHED / ALL HIS POSSESSIONS TO HER CULT, / AFTER HAVING MASTERFULLY PLANNED HER CHURCH. / HE LIVED SEVENTY-TWO YEARS, SIX MONTHS AND SIXTEEN DAYS, / HE DIED MAY 16TH, 1669. / FRANCESCO BARBERINI CARDINAL OF THE HOLY ROMAN CHURCH, / IN MEMORY OF SO MUCH VIRTUE, MADE THIS INSCRIPTION.[42]

However, it was still the desire of Pietro's pupils and followers to pay homage with a more worthy monument in the church, and a tablet chiselled by Luca Berrettini was placed in the *Confessio* in 1675 – after all, over and above the Chapel of St Lazarus, it was this area of the church that was so dear to Pietro: it was here that the reconstruction of the building had obtained the fulcrum of its impetus, and it was here that he had invested so much of his energy, time and money. Luca's tablet summarized the most important passages of Pietro's will, so that they were rendered obvious and memorable to all. However, it is telling that as soon as the tablet was erected, some academicians protested and demanded its immediate removal. They succeeded in this and also asked that those who had installed the offending item without the permission of the Accademia be liable for damaging the walls – in other words, Luca, and Pietro's other supporters were little better than vandals.[43] This reaction stemmed, in part at least, from the fact that the contract between Pietro and the Accademia concerning the original location of his tomb/memorial drafted in 1636 was never officially ratified, despite Pietro's many requests. This contract granted Pietro the patronage of the *Confessio* and the right to be buried there along with anyone he wanted. Pietro himself had also encouraged the academicians to have themselves buried in the *Confessio*, and to build their own memorials there. But they surely feared that, by signing Pietro's contract, the lower church would

Fig. 3.11) View of the main nave of the church and of Pietro da Cortona's tomb.

still become in effect, and notwithstanding the presence of the newly rediscovered saints' relics, Pietro da Cortona's personal mausoleum. If turned into 'Pietro's church', rather than the Accademia's, this would have also diminished the building's effectiveness as a symbol of the Accademia's institutional importance.[44] In addition, in signing this contract, the Accademia would have deprived itself of any legal power over the lower church. In 1666, over 30 years after the contract concerning the patronage of the *Confessio* was drawn up, Pietro was still asking the Accademia to countersign the notarial document, if only as a token of gratitude for his many efforts in the construction of the church as a whole. The answer was once again in the negative, despite the mediation of such eminent academicians as the painter Carlo Maratti (1625-1713) and the painter and critical historian of art Giovanni Pietro Bellori (1613-1696).[45]

Upon Pietro's death in 1669, the Accademia's umpteenth refusal clearly revealed itself as pure obstructionism, and also acted as a counter to anyone who wanted to build a memorial to the late artist in this part of the church. The Accademia now openly exhibited a resentment fuelled by the conditions of Pietro's last will and testament which, in leaving the latter's assets to the lower church and by entrusting their administration to the Congregazione di Santa Eufemia, clearly revealed the deceased's pointed lack of trust in the Accademia itself. Pietro knew that the Accademia was not used to handling large sums of money with any particular care, and that the bequests by two long-deceased members, the painters Girolamo Muziano and Federico Zuccari, had been mismanaged.[46]

By entrusting the management of the *Confessio* to the Congregazione di Santa Eufemia, Pietro da Cortona hoped to protect the lower church (over which he still believed he exercised rights of patronage) from the encroachments of the Accademia. However, it was naïve to suppose that the Accademia would not find some means of having its own way. In 1669, only a few months after Pietro's death, the academicians sealed off the entrance to the lower church with a pair of gates which were installed by way of a 'gift' from Carlo Maratti. It will be recalled that the latter had previously sought to mediate in the dispute between Pietro and the Accademia, and – officially – the gates were meant to safeguard the precious holy ornaments in the *Confessio*.[47] But Maratti's generosity was arguably rather peculiar in nature, and here an overriding allegiance to the interests of the Accademia is possibly revealed: the Accademia had staged a 'take over' of the *Confessio* and could now restrict the chaplains' access to the lower church in a manner that caused considerable friction with the Congregazione di Santa Eufemia. A document reveals that the chaplains of Santa Martina were not able to comply with Pietro's will and were unable to celebrate Mass in the *Confessio* because the Accademia di San Luca withheld the keys that would unlock Maratti's gates. The same document also records that one of the chaplains, a Father Domenico de Santis, openly protested to the Accademia at this obstructionism, and in doing so provoked the following facetious response from Pietro's old antagonist, Bernini: 'Signor Don Domenico, what [Pope] Sixtus [V Peretti] has joined together, let Pietro not separate; we are the owners; show us the concession, if you can'.[48] Of course, Bernini knew that the 'concession' – the 1636 contract that had granted Pietro informal rights of patronage over this space – had never been officially ratified and that, consequently, Pietro's chaplains had no legal power over the *Confessio*.[49] The Accademia then went so far as to lend governance of the sacristy of the lower church of Santa Martina to the sexton of the upper church of San Luca, so that he could effectively turn it into a cellar.[50] With all of this in mind, it is reasonable to assert that some academicians may have long taken advantage of what was probably a sincere enthusiasm and devotion to St Martina on Pietro's part. They let him carry out the construction of the upper and lower church, but upon Pietro's death, they asserted their exclusive jurisdiction over the whole of the building. Quite reasonably, Noehles suggests that the hostility of these academicians was also motivated by envy. Like several artists in the city, Pietro da Cortona had come to Rome young and poor but, *unlike* many others, he had been skilful enough to develop a brilliant career and to become the greatest exponent of a particular species of flamboyant Baroque. He had also become extremely wealthy in the process. Few artists in Rome during this period had ever been blessed with such good fortune.

Naturally, the resistance of certain academicians to an adequate tribute to Pietro da Cortona provoked nothing but scorn among those other members who believed that a proper homage was due. Of course, Pietro's students and admirers, including Ciro Ferri, were part of this faction.[51] In 1677, Ferri showed the Accademia a letter from Cardinal Francesco Barberini, in which the latter ordered the Accademia to allow the restitution of the dedicatory tablet previously removed from the walls of the *Confessio* and to settle all other points of contention, including that involving the sacristy/cellar.[52] Faced with such a peremptory order from the cardinal, the anti-Cortona party had to make the best of a bad situation and satisfy, as much as was possible, the wishes of Cardinal Barberini. Pietro's supporters obviously took utmost advantage of this situation, and erected a brand new tablet (Fig. 3.12). On this occasion, the inscription was composed by Giovanni Pietro Bellori (who was also

Fig. 3.12) Cenotaph of Pietro da Cortona in the *Confessio*.

Fig. 3.13) Cenotaph of Pietro da Cortona in the *Confessio* (detail of Bernardo Fioriti's bust of Pietro da Cortona, c. 1677).

secretary of the Accademia), and the sculptor Bernardo Fioriti (active 1643-1674) was asked to execute a portrait bust of the late Pietro to be placed on top of the tablet (Fig. 3.13).[53] In the spirit of this (not very spontaneous) process of détente, Carlo Maratti again intervened, but this time it was to produce an *Allegorical design in honour of Pietro da Cortona* – a drawing now at Windsor (Inv.904091r) which was meant to celebrate Pietro's memory in laudatory tones. After all, Pietro had provided the Accademia with a remarkable church which increased its prestige – something that Maratti (a strenuous supporter of the Accademia's intellectual and artistic role) must have certainly appreciated. The drawing shows Time sitting on Envy, while holding a profile portrait of Pietro da Cortona. Undoubtedly, and somewhat ironically given his own role in gating off the *Confessio* of the lower church, Maratti wished viewers to mull over the envy Pietro da Cortona had aroused, not only in life (Pascoli also speaks of the jealousy exhibited by artists in Florence), but even after his death.[54]

Conclusion

One is finally left with the following question: why did Pietro put so much of his heart and soul, not to mention his purse, into the (re)creation of the Church of Santi Luca e Martina? In addressing the issue of Pietro's motivations, one has to take into account four distinct aspects of the conundrum. The first involves a religious element: despite the convenience of the discovery of the relics of St Martina, there is no doubt that Pietro da Cortona was a man of great faith, driven by a remarkable religious fervour and one who came to entertain a great devotion to this saint, as his will and his bequest clearly demonstrate. The second aspect, which is intrinsically linked to the religious dimension, concerns Rome's Counter-Reformation culture and the spiritual fervour that flourished in the city, with which Pietro da Cortona was completely aligned. In all likelihood, Pietro's spirituality was also encouraged by his acquaintances, which included strong connections to the Jesuits in Rome. In fact, Pietro co-authored a book with the Jesuit Father Giovanni Domenico Ottonelli (1584-1670), the *Trattato della Pittura, e Scultura, uso ed abuso loro, composto da un Theologo e da un Pittore* (i.e. *Treatise on Painting and Sculpture, on their use and misuse, written by a Theologian and a Painter*), which was published in Florence in 1652, under anagrammatized pseudonyms.[55] The Trattato was intended to enhance the ethical function of the arts, according to the rules established by the Council of Trent. Therefore, if art had an ethical function, the artist had a key role within society since he was a trait d'union – namely a means by which an ethical message was transmitted and became literally visible to the whole of society. Art and the artist therefore had to pursue a noble task of prime importance.[56] As a corollary of this, the third aspect of the conundrum arises from this concept concerning the nobility of art and the artist. It is arguable that all of these beliefs led Pietro to strive intellectually, artistically and economically in the construction of the new church of his professional guild. Moreover, it is likely that, in Pietro da Cortona's mind, the rebuilding of the church was designed to give new dignity to the figure of the artist and the role of art in society. It is arguable that the real reasons for his generosity should be sought more in the realm of those high ideals that transcended the immediate, day-to-day concerns of the Accademia, rather than in any purely self-serving and conceited considerations that one might be tempted to apply to him retrospectively. Furthermore, it is highly unlikely that the low opinion Pietro da Cortona had of some of the Accademia di San Luca's activities would have motivated the dedication with which he carried out this project.

Fourthly, and finally, one should consider that the church of Santi Luca e Martina is the only architectural project entirely designed by Pietro da Cortona, even though he had already overseen the following major projects in and around Rome: the Casino del Pigneto for the Marchese Sacchetti, the façade of Santa Maria della Pace, the façade of Santa Maria in Via Lata, and the dome for the church of San Carlo al Corso. The Casino del Pigneto was a small building in an area situated, at that time, outside Rome, infested by malaria and for that reason little frequented even by the Sacchetti family. As a result, the building designed and built by Pietro fell into ruin. As far as Santa Maria della Pace, Santa Maria in Via Lata, and San Carlo al Corso are concerned, they were partial architectural interventions, inserted into pre-existent structures. So, in the case of the Church of Santi Luca e Martina, the building's beginnings were integral with the designs of Pietro da Cortona. Therefore, this was the first sacred building in Rome entirely designed and built by Pietro, and it was he who also contributed financially to its construction. Is it any wonder that he was particularly attached to a church which, despite those high-minded concerns previously outlined, inevitably meant a great deal in terms of professional prestige and personal satisfaction? With all this in mind, Pietro's wish to be buried in this church – 'his beloved daughter' – was quite reasonable. And it was inevitable that his burial there, no matter how simple and humble, would potentially transform the entire building into a mausoleum devoted to his memory, and this would be at the expense of the academicians of San Luca.[57]

* This essay stems from my IRCHSS-funded doctoral dissertation, completed at University College Dublin, and supervised by Dr Philip Cottrell to whom I wish to express my deep gratitude. I also wish to thank M° Andrea Ceraso for his help in taking the pictures for this paper. As for the translations of the documents cited here, unless otherwise noted, all English translations from Italian and Latin are mine.

[1] For the former church of San Luca on the Esquiline Hill, see Flaminio Vacca, *Memorie di varie antichità trovate in diversi luoghi della città di Roma, scritte da Flaminio Vacca nell'anno 1594* (Rome: Giovanni Lorenzo Barbiellini Libraro a Pasquino, 1741), 245. See also Giovanni Mario Crescimbeni's manuscript, quoted in Vittorio Massimo, *Notizie Istoriche della Villa Massimo alle Terme Diocleziane* (Rome: Tipografia Salviucci, 1836), 93. All of this happened ten years after the Università dei Pittori – a simple craft guild – was transformed into an actual Academy, thanks to the efforts of none other than the painter Girolamo Muziano (c.1528-1592). See Carlo Pietrangeli, 'Origini e vicende dell'Accademia', in *L'Accademia Nazionale di San Luca*, edited by Carlo Pietrangeli (Rome: De Luca, 1974), 10. For the history of the church at the Forum, see Ferruccio Lombardi, *Roma: chiese, conventi, chiostri. Progetto per un inventario, 313-1925* (Rome: Edilstampa, 1993), 230, but also Massimo, *Notizie Istoriche*, 91-92, and especially Karl Noehles, *La chiesa dei SS. Luca e Martina nell'opera di Pietro da Cortona* (Rome: Ugo Bozzi, 1969), 43.

[2] Noehles, *La chiesa dei SS. Luca e Martina*, 41.

[3] For further reading on Federico Zuccari's time as *principe* (1593-1594), see Melchior Missirini, *Memorie per servire alla storia della romana Accademia di S. Luca fino alla morte di Antonio Canova* (Rome: Stamperia De Romanis, 1823), 23-67, and Piera Giovanna Tordella, *La linea del disegno. Teoria e tecnica dal Trecento al Seicento*, Campus (Milan: Bruno Mondadori, 2009), 70. For the rebuilding projects, see Noehles, *La chiesa dei SS. Luca e Martina*, 46.

[4] In 1625, during a pastoral visit, the church was described as virtually beyond repair, since the walls were almost in ruins, the windows had no frames and the roof was in need of serious attention. Noehles, *La chiesa dei SS. Luca e Martina*, 47.

[5] Lombardi, *Roma: chiese, conventi, chiostri*, 230.

[6] See Noehles, *La chiesa dei SS. Luca e Martina*, 83. In 1624, Cardinal Francesco Barberini commissioned Pietro to carry out a cycle of frescoes in the Church of Santa Bibiana in Rome, and in 1626 the same cardinal commissioned an altarpiece from Pietro for the altar of St Erasmus in St Peter's Basilica. *Ibid.*

[7] The tenure of *principe* was elective and would generally last between one and three years, depending on the artist's needs. Bernini, for instance, made it clear that he would accept the appointment on the condition that he would not remain in office above a year. This was probably due to the many commissions with which he had been entrusted. On Bernini's *principato*, see Noehles, 97. However, an artist that had already been *principe* could be elected again – see the case of the Cavalier d'Arpino, elected for the 1615-16 tenure, and in 1629 for a one-year tenure. Only in one case, that of Carlo Maratti, the tenure was for life, following Pope Clement XI's wish. See Angela Cipriani, *Æqua potestas: le arti in gara a Roma nel Settecento* (Rome: De Luca, 2000), 118.

[8] As further evidence of Bernini's efforts to obstruct other artists patronized by the Barberini one can consider his relationship with François Duquesnoy (c.1594-1643) in the context of the sculpture of *St Andrew* in St Peter's, as mentioned in Giovanni Battista Passeri's *Vite de' pittori, scultori, ed architetti che anno lavorato in Roma, morti dal 1641 fino al 1673* (Rome: Vittorio Settari, 1772), 89-

91. According to Passeri, Bernini willingly obstructed Duquesnoy by making his life very difficult, and by constantly changing plans. See also Stanislao Fraschetti, *Il Bernini. La sua vita, la sua opera, il suo tempo* (Milan: Ulrico Hoepli, 1900), 75. As for the relations between Bernini and Pietro da Cortona in the context of architectural projects, see Noehles, *La chiesa dei SS. Luca e Martina*, 88 footnote no.163, but also Tod Allan Marder, 'Rapporti fra Cortona e Bernini architetti', in *Pietro da Cortona: atti del convegno internazionale*, eds Christoph Luitpold Frommel and Sebastian Schütze (Milan: Electa, 1998), 270-78.

[9] Noehles, *La chiesa dei SS. Luca e Martina*, 88.

[10] *Ibid.*

[11] For Pietro's activity as the Barberini court painter, see Anna Lo Bianco, 'Pietro da Cortona e gli anni della volta Berberini', in *I Barberini e la cultura europea del Seicento*, eds Lorenza Mochi Onori, Sebastian Schütze, and Francesco Solinas (Rome: De Luca, 2007), 213-20; but also Lorenza Mochi Onori, 'La piccola galleria e il grande salone di Pietro da Cortona', in *Pietro da Cortona: atti del convegno internazionale*, eds Christoph Luitpold Frommel and Sebastian Schütze (Milan: Electa, 1998), 36-50; and Bruno Zanardi, Anna Lo Bianco, and Orietta Verdi, *Il voltone di Pietro da Cortona in Palazzo Barberini. Con un notiziario*, Quaderni di Palazzo Venezia pubblicati a cura della Soprintendenza per i beni artistici e storici di Roma (Rome: De Luca, 1983), 11-52.

[12] Noehles, *La chiesa dei SS. Luca e Martina*, 97.

[13] *Ibid.* Merz argues that the restoration works, initiated by Pietro da Cortona, are proof that, at the time of his election, he had not yet considered the possibility of reconstructing the church *ex novo*, but only to restore it. Merz adds: 'Cortona's principal idea, however, was to play the Early Christian card, that is, to call attention to the church and its eventual restoration by producing the relics of the titular saint'. Jörg Martin Merz, 'SS. Luca e Martina', in *Pietro da Cortona and Roman Baroque Architecture* (New Haven & London: Yale University Press, 2008), 55.

[14] Noehles, *La chiesa dei SS. Luca e Martina*, 98.

[15] The fact is also mentioned by Giovanni Baglione, *Le vite de' pittori, scultori et architetti dal pontificato di Gregorio XIII del 1572 in fino a' tempi di Papa Urbano Ottavo nel 1642* (Rome: Stamperia d'Andrea Fei, 1642*)*, 169. *Osservazioni sopra i cimiterj de' santi martiri ed antichi cristiani di Roma*, 3 vols., vol. I (Rome: Giovanni Maria Salvioni, 1720), 701.

[16] For the finding of the supposed relics of St Martina, see Donatella Livia Sparti, 'Pietro da Cortona e le presunte reliquie di santa Martina', in *Pietro da Cortona: atti del convegno internazionale*, eds Christoph Luitpold Frommel and Sebastian Schütze (Milan: Electa, 1998), 243-55, who argues that the relics may have not been authentic, just as the pseudo-paleo-Christian inscriptions on the sarcophagi have been proved to be a 16th-17th centuries fake.

[17] See Marsilio Honorati, *Historia di Santa Martina vergine e martire romana cavata da gl'antichi manuscritti, con alcune annotationi, e consideratini sopra di essa* (Rome: Francesco Cavalli, 1635), 102-07, but also Liliana Barroero, 'Testa reliquiario di santa Martina', in *Pietro da Cortona: 1597-1669*, exh. cat. ed. by Anna Lo Bianco, (Rome, Palazzo Venezia, 1997), 450.

[18] Noehles, *La chiesa dei SS. Luca e Martina*, 99.

[19] See Jennifer Montagu, 'Apparizione della Vergine con il Bambino a santa Martina', in *Pietro da Cortona: 1597-1669*, 441, as well as Oreste Ferrari and Serenita Papaldo, *Le sculture del Seicento a Roma* (Rome: Ugo Bozzi, 1999), 192-93. The permit for the construction of the memorial in the *Confessio* occurred in 1636, with a notarial document eventually never signed by academicians. The

document is in the Archivio di Stato di Roma, Silvestro Spada, 'Die X Januaris 1636. Concessio Confessionis in Ecclesia SS. Luca et Martina Pro Ill. D. Pietro Cortoniensis', in *Trenta Notai Capitolini, Ufficio 31, Notaio Silvestro Spada* (1636), 66 et seq., 93 et seq. The document is also quoted in Donatella Livia Sparti, *La casa di Pietro da Cortona: architettura, accademia, atelier e officina* (Rome: F.lli Palombi, 1997), 21, and in Jörg Martin Merz, 'Ss. Luca e Martina reconsidered', in *Pietro da Cortona: atti del convegno internazionale*, eds Christoph Luitpold Frommel and Sebastian Schütze (Milan: Electa, 1998), 241. Noehles also transcribed the document, but only partially. See Noehles, *La chiesa dei SS. Luca e Martina*, 100. As for the relics, the sarcophagi in which the saints were reinterred were probably the products of Niccolò Menghini's workshop. Menghini was also commissioned to execute a statue of Santa Martina which was placed on the high altar in the autumn of 1635. Noehles, *La chiesa dei SS. Luca e Martina*, 100-01.

[20] Noehles, *La chiesa dei SS. Luca e Martina*, 103.

[21] Ibid., 103.

[22] As well as supervising the construction yard, and the execution of works in stucco and marble in the lower church, Luca Berrettini was also put in charge of erecting the large bronze altar above the tomb of the martyrs. *Ibid.*, 104. The bronze altar was entirely paid by Pietro da Cortona. See Lione Pascoli, *Vite de' pittori, scultori ed architetti moderni*, 2 vols., vol. I (Rome: Antonio de' Rossi nella strada del Seminario Romano, 1730), 8.

[23] Noehles, *La chiesa dei SS. Luca e Martina*, 104. See also Pascoli, *Vite de' pittori*, 7. For Pietro da Cortona's stay in Florence, see Giuliano Briganti, 'Pietro Berrettini (Pietro da Cortona)', in *Dizionario Biografico degli Italiani* (Rome: Istituto della Enciclopedia italiana, 1967), 398-405. For further reading on the Camera della Stufa, see Walter Vitzthum and Malcolm Campbell, 'Pietro da Cortona's Camera della Stufa', in *The Burlington Magazine* CIV, no. 708 (1962), 120-25, whereas for Pietro's activity in Palazzo Pitti, see Walter Vitzthum, 'Pietro da Cortona's Drawings for the Pitti Palace at the Uffizi', in *The Burlington Magazine* CVII, no. 751 (1965), 522-26, but also Susan Russell, 'Pietro da Cortona's Drawings of "Minerva" for the Sala di Giove in the Palazzo Pitti', in *Master Drawings* XXXIV, no. 3 (1996), 303-08. As far as Ferdinando II's life and patronage is concerned, see Irene Cotta Stumpo, 'Ferdinando II de' Medici, granduca di Toscana', in *Dizionario Biografico degli Italiani* (Rome: Istituto della Enciclopedia italiana, 1996), 278-283.

[24] Noehles, *La chiesa dei SS. Luca e Martina*, 105.

[25] For further reading on Pope Innocent X, see Olivier Poncet, 'Innocenzo X papa', in *Dizionario Biografico degli Italiani* (Rome: Istituto della Enciclopedia italiana, 2004), 466-78 and respective bibliography.

[26] For the Barberini and Innocent X's accusation of embezzlement, see Alberto Merola, 'Francesco Barberini', in *Dizionario Biografico deli Italiani* (Rome: Istituto della Enciclopedia italiana, 1964), 172-76, and Claudio Rendina, *I papi: storia e segreti*, Grandi tascabili contemporanei (Rome: Newton Compton, 2011), 685.

[27] Noehles, *La chiesa dei SS. Luca e Martina*, 105.

[28] Ibid.

[29] For further reading on the reconciliation between the Barberini and the Pamphilj, see Francesco Cancellieri, *Il mercato, il lago dell'acqua vergine, ed il Palazzo Panfiliano nel Circo Agonale detto volgarmente Piazza Navona*, (Rome: Francesco Bourlie, 1811), 110.

[30] Noehles, *La chiesa dei SS. Luca e Martina*, 105.

[31] *Ibid.*, 107.
[32] Unfortunately, there are no archival documents that may shed new light as to when, and under what conditions, the patronage of this chapel was granted to Pietro. Noehles suggests that the patronage was granted to him because Cardinal Francesco Barberini was no longer willing to pay for further construction work, and Pietro, as a patron of the chapel, was the only one responsible for its construction costs. *Ibid.*, 106-07.
[33] *Ibid.*, 109.
[34] *Ibid.*
[35] *Ibid.*, 108.
[36] *Ibid.* The finishing touches were applied between the 18th and the 19th centuries. However, the façade, designed by Pietro, was never completed in its entirety because of the death of the last of the church's great sponsors, Cardinal Francesco Barberini, in 1679. An impression of the intended façade is supplied by an engraving by Giovanni Battista Falda (c.1640-1678), illustrated in *Il nuovo teatro delle fabriche, et edificii, in prospettiva di Roma moderna: sotto il felice pontificato di N. S. Papa Alessandro VII* (Rome: Giovanni Giacomo Rossi, 1655-1699), who was obviously aware of the original project designs. What currently exists would, in fact, have constituted the furthest protruding part of the entire façade.
[37] The Confraternita di San Giuseppe di Terrasanta, commonly dubbed the Congregazione dei Virtuosi al Pantheon, was a confraternity of artists housed at the Church of Santa Maria ad Martyres. As a result of their artistic skill, they were dubbed the Congregazione dei Virtuosi at the Pantheon. For further reading, see Vitaliano Tiberia, *La Compagnia di S. Giuseppe di Terrasanta nel XVI secolo*, (Galatina: Congedo, 2000). As for Pietro da Cortona's funeral, see Archivio di Stato di Roma, Anonymous, 'Funerale della b.me. del S. Pietro Berrettino da Cortona', in *Archivio del Conservatorio di Santa Eufemia* (1669), 21. The document has also been transcribed by Noehles, 365.
[38] See Montagu, 'Apparizione della Vergine con il Bambino a santa Martina', 441, also Ferrari and Papaldo, *Le sculture del Seicento*, 192-93, and Elena Bianca Di Gioia, Apparizione della Vergine con il Bambino a santa Martina', in R*accolte della città di Perugia: Collezione Valentino Martinelli*, exh. cat. eds Francesco Federico Mancini, Elena Bianca Di Gioia, and Daniela Gallavotti Cavallero, (Perugia: Palazzo della Penna, 2002), 95.
[39] See Noehles, *La chiesa dei SS. Luca e Martina*, 111, but also Merz, 'SS. Luca e Martina', 77.
[40] Archivio di Stato di Roma, Pietro Berrettini da Cortona, 'Testamento e codicilli di Pietro da Cortona', in *Trenta Notai Capitolini*, Ufficio 1, Notaio Angiolucci (1669), ad datam. The document has also been published by Giuseppe Coceva, 'Il testamento di Pietro da Cortona', Archivio Storico dell'Arte III, no. 5/6 (1890), 210-13.
[41] 'Also, I leave and grant the above Church of Santa Martina (but not as united to S. Luca, in fact separate from the Accademia di San Luca ...) 6˙750 *scudi* in different bonds I possess ..., and the fruits of these bonds ... must serve exclusively to fulfil the following obligations, and not otherwise under any pretext, even if [the pretext was] useful to the same Church of Santa Martina'. *Ibid.*
[42] Pascoli, *Vite de' pittori*, 11-13.
[43] *Ibid.*, 110-12.
[44] *Ibid.*, 339-40, 44. See also Merz, 'SS. Luca e Martina', 61, and Sparti, *La casa di Pietro da Cortona: architettura, accademia, atelier e officina*, 21.

[45] Merz, 'SS. Luca e Martina', 69-70. This legal ambivalence, caused by the existence of both a non-signed contract, and an oral agreement between Pietro and the Accademia, gave rise to a legal controversy between the Accademia di San Luca and the Conservatorio di Santa Eufemia, aimed at clarifying who was entitled to the patronage of the lower church. The litigation lasted more than two centuries. The Conservatorio di Santa Eufemia is still the owner of the lower church, whereas the upper church belongs to the Accademia. The archival documents relating to this legal matter are in the Archive of the Accademia di San Luca, and in the Archive of the Conservatorio of Santa Eufemia (now at the Archivio di Stato in Rome).

[46] Noehles, *La chiesa dei SS. Luca e Martina*, 111.

[47] *Ibid.*, 356.

[48] 'Signor Don Domenico, Sixtus coniunxit, Petrus non separet; siamo noi li padroni; mostri, se puole, la concessione'. *Ibid.*, 358. The document, quoted by Noehles, is one of the many in the Archivio del Conservatorio di Santa Eufemia, today at the Archivio di Stato in Rome.

[49] Giuseppe Vasi (1710-1782) recounts that when Bernini saw Pietro's design for the Casino del Pigneto, commissioned by the Marchese Sacchetti (1589-1648), he regarded them as too small, and sarcastically remarked: 'Petruccio wants to build a nativity scene [Petruccio vuol fare un presepio]'. Giuseppe Vasi, *Delle magnificenze di Roma antica e moderna. Libro decimo che contiene le ville e giardini più rimarchevoli*, 10 vols., vol. X (Rome: Niccolò e Marco Pagliarini mercanti di libri a Pasquino, 1761), 11.

[50] Noehles, *La chiesa dei SS. Luca e Martina*, 112. The division in titular dedication is not defined by upper and lower church. Indeed, the issue of the division of the two churches stemmed from Pietro who – in leaving the money to the lower church of Santa Martina – created a division problem that never existed in churches with double dedication.

[51] *Ibid.*

[52] The tablet was left in the church backyard for about two years. *Ibid.*

[53] Lione Pascoli, *Vite de' pittori, scultori ed architetti moderni*, 2 vols., vol. II (Rome: Antonio de' Rossi nella strada del Seminario Romano, 1736), 421. Francesco Petrucci suggests that the bust by Bernardo Fioriti – which the scholar Nicholas Turner considers rather poor – is derived from Pietro da Cortona's *Self-portrait* at the Uffizi. See Francesco Petrucci, 'Papi e architettie', in *Roma barocca: Bernini, Borromini, Pietro da Cortona*, exh. cat. eds by Maurizio Fagiolo and Paolo Portoghesi (Rome: Museo nazionale di Castel Sant'Angelo, 2006), 103, and Nicholas Turner, 'Portraits of Pietro da Cortona', in *Pietro da Cortona: atti del convegno internazionale*, eds Christoph Luitpold Frommel and Sebastian Schütze (Milan: Electa, 1998), 12, but also Merz, 'SS. Luca e Martina', 77.

[54] Pascoli, *Vite de' pittori*, 6.

[55] See Gauvin Alexander Bailey, '"Le style jésuite n'existe pas". Jesuit Corporate Culture and the Visual Arts', in *The Jesuits: Cultures, Sciences, and the Arts, 1540-1773*, eds John W. O'Malley and others (Toronto: University of Toronto Press, 1999), 68. This *Trattato* is clearly inspired by the Counter-Reformation principles in matters of art, and it very much reflects the theories of Cardinal Gabriele Paleotti stated in the book *Discorso intorno alle immagini sacre e profane*, published in Bologna in 1582.

[56] See Julius Schlosser Magnino, *La letteratura artistica. Manuale delle fonti della storia dell'arte moderna*, eds Julius Schlosser Magnino and Otto Kurz, trans. Filippo Rossi (Florence: La Nuova Italia, 1967), 616-17, but also Noehles, *La chiesa dei SS. Luca e Martina*, 4.

[57] Pascoli, *Vite de' pittori*, 12. Besides Pietro da Cortona, other artists were buried in the upper church of San Luca. These include the architect Adriano Rainaldi (†1597), the painter and architect Tommaso Laureti (c.1530-1602), the architect Ottaviano Mascherino (1524-1606), the painter Antonio Circignani (c.1567-1629), the architect Girolamo Rainaldi (1524-1606, son of Adriano), the sculptor Giuliano Finelli (c.1601-1653, Gianlorenzo Bernini's famous assistant), the artist Lazzaro Baldi (c.1624-1703), the architect Giambattista Sorìa (1581-1651) and the painter Giovanna Garzoni (1600-1670). For the events concerning the old seat of the Accademia di San Luca, formerly adjacent to the Church before the demolition in the 1930s, see Isabella Salvagni, 'The Unversità dei Pittori and the Accademia di San Luca from the installation in San Luca sull'Esquilino to the reconstruction of Santa Martina al Foro Romano', in *The Accademia Seminars: the Accademia di San Luca in Rome, c. 1590-1635*, ed. Peter M. Lukehart (Washington D.C.: National Gallery of Art, 2009), 69-121, but also Isabella Salvagni, 'Pour l'histoire de l'Académie de Saint-Luc. Notes pour une révision', in *Revue de l'art* CLXXI, no. 1 (2011), 17-29, and Isabella Salvagni, 'La chiesa dei santi Luca e Martina ai Fori Imperiali e l'Accademia di San Luca. Dall'Universitas all'Accademia: Istituzione e sedi tra primo Cinquecento e gli anni Trenta del Novecento' (Ph.D. Dissertation, Università degli Studi Roma Tre, 2005), passim.

4 | How Tocqueville became 'Tocqueville'

Gustave the Beaumont's Letters from Cannes and the First Edition of *Memoir, Letters, and Remains of Alexis de Tocqueville*

Andreas Hess

In his article 'How to become an iconic social thinker' Dominik Bartmanski has tried to analyse how some twentieth century intellectuals achieved iconic status. He argues that three factors are crucial: (1) liminal time, by which he means the specific moment that creates the cultural space that allows for intellectual creativity; (2) charisma, by which he means not a God-given quality or status but something that is linked to performance; and (3) a cultural coding, a kind of theoretical rhetoric that it closer to the sacred than the profane in the sense that it formulates the questions of our times, identifies the major currents in our society and formulates an entire program or paradigm that needs pursuing.[1] Bartmanski concludes that there is no recipe for how to become an iconic social thinker; only hindsight allows the social scientist to identify some factors, and what can be said with hindsight is that contingencies do play a major role. However, such circumstances and historical constellations are notoriously hard to reconstruct *post festum*.

In what follows I will try to use the example of Gustave de Beaumont and Alexis de Tocqueville to show that the process by which one becomes an iconic thinker has a few more variables built in than described by Bartmanski. For example, while contingency plays a major role, the creation of icons relies sometimes also on willed performances and involves some form of intent and planning. Furthermore, if Jeffrey Alexander's definition is correct that 'icons are symbolic condensations' and that 'they root generic, social meanings in a specific and "material" form' and that 'they allow the abstraction of morality to be subsumed, to be made indivisible, by aesthetic shape'[2] then we need to understand the process through which this happens. Alexander himself suggests that this is mainly through '"feeling", by contact, by the "evidence of the senses" rather than the mind'. He notes further that 'the iconic is about experience, not communication'.[3] While such ideal-type juxtaposition might help to explain some general features of iconicity, I suggest that the very process of icon-construction itself is about both communication *and* lived experience. It makes reference to a specific communicative performance that makes us believe in the singular experience that an icon or the life of an icon holds. This is particularly true if there is more than one person involved in the making of an icon. While the cases of Boswell and Hume (and Dr. Johnson) or Engels and Marx could prove to be instructive in this regard, the case I am interested in here is that of Alexis de Tocqueville and Gustave de Beaumont, and particularly how Beaumont came to terms with Tocqueville's death. My hypothesis is that Beaumont succeeded in the latter attempt ultimately because he managed to create and to evoke the ur-image of Tocqueville, that is, by showing him as a man of admirable qualities who managed partly to transcend his own limitations, yet without turning Tocqueville into some superhuman Nietzschean figure.

To most people Tocqueville is known as the author of *Democracy in America*, the 'sphinx' who predicted not only the emergence of modern democracy but who was also brilliant in predicting what was likely to happen to it, including its self-destructing qualities – and nothing better than a thinker whose predictions turned out to be spot on on more than one occasion! However, Tocqueville did not become an honorary American, a sort of intellectual Founding Father and a classic democratic theorist overnight. Only a few readers outside academia, perhaps only those interested in Tocquevilliana, will have heard of Tocqueville's travelling companion, co-writer and friend Gustave de Beaumont. Yet, it is largely thanks to Beaumont's efforts that Tocqueville could become 'Tocqueville'.

What I intend to do in this essay is not to go through the secondary literature or the Tocqueville reception in general; rather, my intention is to sketch out how Tocqueville achieved early iconic status.[4] In order to do so I will look at the complex process of how Beaumont convinced himself that the remembrance of Tocqueville was absolutely crucial, that his legacy needed to be preserved and that it was his task to do exactly that. Looking at the concrete circumstances under which such a decision is made it becomes clear that it is the struggle that Tocqueville goes through towards the end of his life that makes Beaumont reflect about the deeper, almost metaphysical search for the meaning of Tocqueville's life. The struggle for his life was not something that was tangential to the man's work; *au contraire*, Beaumont becomes convinced – or better, is convincing himself – that the human and moral qualities of Tocqueville, including his final struggle, are not something that can be separated from his *oeuvre*. Alexander is right to insist that icons are first and foremost symbolic condensations. For Beaumont this practically means that he must show that there was some homology if not to say unity between his work and the personality of the man. However, in contrast to Alexander I also believe that no iconicity project is viable without some real material substance – such as a moral life, for example, and the capacity to transcend or to look beyond the circumstances one finds oneself in. For the icon-building process the three aspects of work – personality – morals must be understood as being co-existential and dependent on each other; together they form more than the sum of its parts .

Having said that the search for meaning gets even more complicated because for Beaumont an additional factor is important, and that is his proximity to and friendship with Tocqueville. In earlier letters that were exchanged between Beaumont and Tocqueville a number of passages can be encountered in which Beaumont expresses his admiration for Tocqueville and admits his friend's intellectual superiority.[5] However, it is only while sitting at Tocqueville's deathbed that Beaumont decides to do everything to preserve his friend's memory and work. Both his admiration for his friend and his dependency on him were the crucial points and give meaning to Beaumont's own performance after Tocqueville's death. This can be best detected in his almost daily dispatches from Tocqueville's deathbed in Cannes to his wife Clémentine in which he reports minutely the declining health of his friend.

Beaumont's letters do not reveal some weird necrophile interest in how a great man dies but instead must be understood as important markers of a development in which Beaumont convinces himself of the necessity to preserve his friend's legacy. This search for meaning for both his own life and that of his friend finds its prolongation in a memoir, which in fact turns out to be the first biography of Tocqueville ever published in both France and America, together with the publication of some of the more personal writings and impressions of Tocqueville.[6] It is basically through these editorial efforts that Beaumont is able to create 'Tocqueville', the intellectual icon. In doing so, Beaumont manages to create a lasting imagery of Tocqueville, not by portraying him as superhuman but by sketching Tocqueville as a normal human being driven mainly by intellectual curiosity and moral judgment. Thus Tocqueville gets introduced to the newly developing public sphere not as an intellectual giant who wrote *Democracy in America*, but first and foremost as a charismatic person who came to terms with the challenging questions of his time. That Beaumont also benefited from the proximity to the great intellectual undertaking and from the friendship to Tocqueville is an interesting side effect. However, it would be going too far to suggest that that was actually the prime intention. It would also conflict with those aristocratic values of selflessness and humility that the two Frenchmen were brought up with. Be it selflessness, duty to friendship or enlightened self-interest, what I will mainly argue is that we are confronted here with an extraordinary case of dual performativity.

Beaumont's Letters from Cannes

Towards the end of 1858 Alexis de Tocqueville, suffering from respiratory and lung problems, had been advised to spend some time away from both the damp and cold estate in Normandy and his home in Paris. Accompanied by his wife Marie and his brother Hippolyte, Tocqueville sought refuge in a villa on the outskirts of Cannes. Despite some signs of improvement due to the warmer Mediterranean climate it soon became clear that Tocqueville was in a worse condition than originally assumed: he was suffering from severe tuberculosis, which affected his right lung and, as a secondary result, also his throat. Over the next few weeks and months signs of improvement and hope mixed with physical and mental crises.

Tocqueville, who suspected that his illness was even more serious, begged his friend Gustave de Beaumont to join him in Cannes. Beaumont obliged, despite experiencing serious financial trouble with his own estate at Beaumont La Chartre. Beaumont arrived in Cannes on 11 March 1859 and spent the next few weeks at what would eventually turn out to be Tocqueville's deathbed. During his stay he sent regular detailed reports back to his wife Clémentine. In these letters from Cannes[7] Beaumont not only reported on his friend's last struggle but also began to reflect about Tocqueville's achievements, his personal relationships with his brothers, his wife and various friends, thus providing us with a touching, human character portrait of the public intellectual and author of *Democracy in America*.

Writing these intimate, sometimes painful letters, turned out to be the beginning of a longer period of intense reflection, a period that would eventually result in Beaumont's memoirs of Tocqueville, which, together with the first collection of Tocqueville's unpublished letters and works, laid the foundations on which much of the later reception, celebration and reputation of Tocqueville would rest.[8] This process of reputation building, however, was a subtle process in that it was most certainly not as consciously willed as it might appear to a later observer. The Cannes letters describe the late Tocqueville, who had often been regarded as cold and distant – allegedly the German poet Heinrich Heine regarded Tocqueville as such a person – more as a very humble and human person. That impression was also maintained in Beaumont's memoirs of Tocqueville. The 'trick' was that Beaumont humanized Tocqueville while at the same time portraying him as having an exceptional mind and being a prime thinker who was the first to systematically reflect on the conditions of modern democracy. Taken together, the Cannes letters about a dying man and Beaumont's memoirs, together with the first edition of Tocqueville's letters and other unpublished writings, laid the foundations on which Tocqueville's later iconic reputation would come to rest. In other words, it is due to Beaumont's letters, his memoirs and his editorial work that Tocqueville became the Tocqueville we know today.

The first hint that Tocqueville's condition was more serious than previously thought appeared in a letter that Beaumont wrote *en route* from Paris to his wife Clémentine who had remained at the family's estate. In a short paragraph Beaumont notes: 'I am most annoyed! You will not receive any news from Cannes. No-one here has any as recent as ours. This silence is very ominous: what to think of it? What sadness!'[9] In a second letter sent from Paris only a few days later Beaumont confessed again his preoccupation with the state his friend was obviously in: 'One thing keeps me busy ...: the health of poor Tocqueville, of whom we have received nothing'.[10] In the same letter Beaumont revealed, however, that through Alexis's sister in law, who received daily communications from her husband Hippolyte, who happened to be at Alexis' bedside in Cannes, he had learned that Tocqueville's condition was indeed serious and included spitting blood and prolonged periods of long silence, the latter probably due to the doctors' advice. Beaumont also reported that Tocqueville needed to be continuously nursed and that two nuns were at his bedside.[11] While Tocqueville's doctors in Cannes, Dr Sève and Dr Maure, checked the patient regularly, and while Tocqueville's wife Marie and his brother Hippolyte were present, the situation was complicated by the fact that nobody dared to reveal to the patient how serious his condition was. This was partly due to some, however limited, hope that all parties shared, particularly on days when Tocqueville seemed to have made some progress and appeared to be in a better condition.

In the weeks and months before the illness had demanded a change of location, Tocqueville had repeatedly tried to calm down his relations and friends, including Beaumont. In reassuring letters he had told friends and family that the anticipated retreat to a warmer climate was to help him in curing what he thought was bronchitis. However, having experienced many severe coughing attacks and after his general condition seemed to have weakened considerably in the months of January and February, Tocqueville began to appear to be more worried, suspecting perhaps that not all was well. This feeling was exacerbated by his own wife's apparent frailty – she had been unable to carry out the most urgent tasks and relied on the two nuns to take care of the patient's immediate care – and the lack of any stimulating conversation, which gave him a sense of disconnectedness from the world's political events.[12] As a busy man Tocqueville's brother Hippolyte could not always be at his bedside to feed him information.

It was under these circumstances that Tocqueville decided to write to Beaumont, requesting his friend's visit.[13] To be sure, it wasn't the first time that Beaumont had been asked to take care of his old friend. Twice before, first when travelling in America in 1831 and, secondly, during their stay in Algeria in 1841, Beaumont had nursed his friend. This third time, however, it turned out to be a more serious matter. After an 18 hour journey Beaumont arrived in Cannes on 11 March. A day later he writes in his first report to Clémentine a rather skeptical note:

> I do not know whether my first impressions deceive me, but I have, alas, been deeply saddened by them ... it is that not only was my journey here justified; but it was necessary. We feared that Alexis' wish to see me was overzealous and mere friendly flattery. I assure you that it is scarcely possible to maintain this fear ... My arrival alone caused him such emotion that he was unable to speak to me for some moments, finding only tears and sobs to show his joy at seeing me. Just now he was telling me that he felt himself to be dying of sadness and isolation. And that in coming I had saved his life ... Alas! Will we save his life?[14]

While the weeks before had seen some progress – Tocqueville had even been able to write letters – at the time Beaumont arrived the patient's condition had worsened again and there seemed to be little or no hope of making a full recovery. 'The current condition', notes Beaumont, 'despite all its perils, is an immense improvement with regard to the situation six weeks ago. He was evidently on the edge of the tomb; today there is a return towards life; but with what a lot of complications'.[15] It became evident over the next few days that Gustave's visit was not going to last just a few days. He got increasingly drawn into the daily planning and procedures, and he even began to take over some of the household duties from Tocqueville's wife, while the immediate care and bedside duties were left to the two nuns.

There were days when Beaumont despaired – so bad was the situation of his friend. There were also days when Tocqueville's wife could not speak because of her own frailty, which was, as the doctor confirmed, due to mental exhaustion, and Beaumont had to pass on her messages to Tocqueville on a slate. Intermittently there were also better days. In another letter to Clémentine Beaumont writes:

> During the day time still passes: mornings are spent on the primary care needed by the invalid. The vesicatories and

cauteries covering his back are bandaged, the doctor visits, and lunch takes place. Then come some little walks, favored by the good weather, and that the invalid takes with pleasure and finishes – unless, like the day before yesterday, his strength fails him completely. He regained them [sic] yesterday ... Around 3 o'clock the post arrives, and newspapers, letters; and then from 4 to 5 some callers, who are received when we feel up to it, and who in any case constitute a light distraction. Dinner at 6 o'clock – up to here we are working well, and there is still an impression of life; but come evening it is like a grave. During the day Madame de Tocqueville sometimes reads aloud and her husband listens with pleasure ... sometimes we must forego the resource of the readings, when the invalid's state of fatigue makes it impossible for him to listen.[16]

After such a tiring day, with very little or no hope of long-term improvement, Beaumont asked himself how long he or anyone could hold out 'against the absolute silence'.[17] The situation got even worse when Tocqueville began to suspect that he was being deprived of information regarding his own condition.

To add to this stressful situation, due to family and professional commitments Tocqueville's brothers were not entirely free to spend long periods in Cannes at his bedside, which left Beaumont with the precarious task of taking care of both Alexis and his wife. This was a major and difficult task, particularly when one takes into account that at the same time the situation in la Sarthe also needed Beaumont's continuous presence. As Beaumont notes, for him the demands were almost impossible to meet: Tocqueville needed both a full-time qualified carer, preferably a doctor, but also somebody who could function as a secretary and intellectual stimulus, 'somebody who can read to him' or 'take down dictation'.[18]

By now – it was the middle of March – Beaumont sent out daily letters, minuting his friend's deteriorating condition. The letters describe the constant and almost daily oscillation between despair and hope, often within one paragraph. Here is an example in which Beaumont describes the patient's impatience, and the will to return to a workable condition and the impending realization that it was not to be, something that not only frustrated Tocqueville but also those around him:

> Maybe we will be moving into a better thing; if this good chance that the doctor considered as being possible were to be realized it would doubtless be at that time that the best would transpire;

and with a return to health would come a more tolerable mental disposition [Beaumont refers here to Tocqueville's impatience]. This condition causes great pity; but one is disheartened by the idea of the little we are capable of against such an ailment; and one feels consumed by more or less sterile efforts. What follows takes away all strength: that is the thought of the <u>immensity</u> of the true ailment, very much greater that the invalid believes he has; it is the <u>slimness</u> of the chances of success ... I struggle, I must assure you, against these impressions with the greatest possible self-control so that I might be sure that our poor friends do not see any hint; and I act as though I had complete confidence in the future.[19]

Only a day later Beaumont seemed totally resigned to the fact that nothing positive could be done. He notes: 'The present state of affairs will kill him in a given time, if it continues; it is with good reason that it is called Consumption; for there is a daily dwindling of strength, without any corresponding restoration'.[20] In the same letter Beaumont confesses that he didn't find it easy to reveal to his friend the full truth about his condition. It must have been particularly painful for Beaumont to see his friend's capacity to judge for himself failing. Beaumont had always admired Tocqueville's hard-headed style of analysis and his critical insight into and judgment of himself and other people. Now he had to realize that his friend was unable to assess his own terminal condition; instead Tocqueville blamed his situation on the proscribed treatment: 'We still succeed in deceiving him; but will we be able to do so forever? He harangued me yesterday (in hushed tones of course) <u>against his doctor</u>, in whom he said he was only <u>half confident</u>'.[21] It was equally painful that Tocqueville's mental activities and interests were also weakening: 'I see him languishing now: unable to read on his own; unable to listen even to short readings'.[22] For somebody who had been regarded almost as the incarnation of intellectual interest and engagement, the soul of reasoning and bookishness such signs were deeply discouraging.

In the letters to his wife Beaumont often returns to the tense relationship between Marie and Alexis, which, under the stressful situation, he found very disheartening. Beaumont became the person both would confide in. For him this must have been an impossible situation to be in. Particularly when Marie sought help he almost felt he was betraying his friend:

> She is absolutely discouraged, worn out, exhausted, overwhelmed; and unfortunately a little detached from her

poor husband, whose condition has taken more strength from her than she could give. She spoke to me with despair of her desire to be dead; it is her desire to escape everything; she sees her husband ardently wishing to live; all her own desire is to see him come to an end before he crushes her, and so she wants no more truck with her husband's surfeit of life, to which he attends so much value.[23]

Forgivingly Beaumont adds that she doesn't know what she is talking about, so consumed is she by watching her husband struggling for his life. He also suspected an 'air of religious duty'. Marie had always been more inclined to follow and practise her religious faith than her husband had been. On the other hand Tocqueville didn't understand his wife's partial withdrawal, and he needed the advice of his friend to explain the circumstances to him: 'I tried to make him understand that from the point of view of his own interests. He must leave her be a little, so as to allow her to regain her strength during the hours of respite and renew her supplies of energy for the days of great crisis which may return'.[24]

A few days after such confessions Tocqueville showed again signs of slight improvement. Yet, these moments were a mere flickering of hope. The rare moments, which seemed like progress, turned the few evenings of readings, like that of Flaubert's *Madame Bovary*, into a passing entertainment pleasure. However, when Tocqueville expressed soon after, and very much against all realistic chances and hope, the wish to continue working on a second volume on his *Ancien Régime* book, Beaumont realized that this would never happen. Unable to 'explain to himself why the convalescence is not more complete, he is always asking why everything is returning so slowly'.[25] He had not to wait for long for the next crisis moment, and after having coughed blood again even Tocqueville himself began to wonder whether the end was coming.

The coughing and spitting indicated that Tocqueville's lung was under attack again. At the same time the doctors still remained reluctant to tell the patient the seriousness of his condition. Beaumont confessed to Clémentine how sad it made him to observe how somebody who all his life had been looking for rational explanations and causes was now being duped. Beaumont sensed that his friend Tocqueville didn't trust the doctors either, which was also one of the main reasons why he continued to ask the current team to be replaced by a 'secretary-cum-doctor'. Beaumont couldn't agree more; Tocqueville needed both 'durable and permanent assistance – at once medical and mental – to be part of their [the couple's] life and household'.[26]

However, finding the right person in such short time proved to be impossible – the main reason Beaumont stayed put with his friend and his wife. The decision to stay became even more pertinent since Tocqueville's condition started to worsen again. Beaumont gives a vivid account of how bad his friend's condition had become. Tocqueville now had trouble 'to find a position that made his sufferings less intolerable ... I heard loud sounds emanating from his chest area and he had an absolute repugnance for all manner of foods'.[27] Beaumont concludes 'Our poor friend, it must be admitted must be in the last stages'. He adds: 'two or three times already, on the face of this poor friend I have glimpsed <u>the fatal claws of death</u>'. Tocqueville's struggle, he writes, was 'no longer a matter <u>of months</u>'; instead he may only 'have weeks'.[28]

Beaumont was surely worried about the outcome, but what repeatedly troubled him was to see that Tocqueville himself seemed not to realize what was happening to him. Still, even at this advanced stage, the doctors did not dare to reveal to the patient the full diagnosis, yet they talked openly about it to Beaumont: 'Dr Maure said to me ... "his condition is hopeless; no healing is possible; his lung is just a wide wound; consumption is continuous and rapid; ... the most favourable chance he has is for this to drag on for a few weeks"'.[29] To this Beaumont commented in resigned fashion that:

> although I recognized the good intentions that dictate the doctor's use of these two contradictory manners of speaking; although I even recommend their great utility to the poor invalid, who would be killed outright by the sight of the truth; it nonetheless always causes me profoundly sad feeling, the staging of this play, that shows with what ease poor humanity is deceived, up to the supreme moment of greatest need for truth. It is impossible to conceive of the depth of his deception. Yesterday again, he said to me 'the good thing about my condition is that, <u>as far as my chest</u> and bronchi <u>are concerned</u>, I am completely healed.'[30]

Beaumont also noted that Madame de Tocqueville was equally deceived, which worried him and burdened his conscience.

Beaumont himself now realized that the end was imminent and that with it a lifelong friendship was also coming to an end: 'If some devotion is needed, I will find resources for it in the very lively feeling of my old friendship'.[31] Beaumont's letters to his wife clearly had a cathartic effect. Support arrived on 4 April, as Beaumont noted in his last letter from Cannes. Tocqueville's brother Eduard and his wife had decided to move from Nice to Cannes and to take over from Beaumont. This was a big relief; Beaumont could go back to his family and estate, which were so urgently awaiting him. Beaumont's intention for his homeward journey had been to pass first through Paris to keep looking for a suitable doctor-cum-secretary. However, this proved futile because the situation in Cannes had turned for the worse. Louis de Kergorlay, Tocqueville's other close friend, and Tocqueville's brother Hippolyte had been asked to come urgently to Cannes. Beaumont took this to mean that death was imminent; after all, it turned out to be 'the day after the one when Tocqueville would have taken communion'.[32]

A few days later some papers prematurely reported Tocqueville's death. On 16 April reliable news came through that Tocqueville had actually died. The same day Beaumont, who during the difficult time in Cannes had found great support in his wife, wrote to her: 'We must give up the idea that we can be happy apart; when we are together we may sometimes have sorrows and difficulties, but never lack the basis of happiness'.[33] Seen retrospectively, the same applies to the friendship between Beaumont and Tocqueville. Death had put an end to that friendship, and the survivor was now faced with the almost insurmountable task of giving meaning to both Tocqueville as a thinker and as a friend and human being. This link between man and work is crucial if one wants to understand the iconic quality of Tocqueville, particularly at a time when taking a moral stance was in high demand. It is perhaps no mere coincidence that in America (which the Boston edition of Tocqueville's scattered writings clearly wanted to reach) a unity of purpose in life was especially called for as the country, which Tocqueville, the democratic prophet, had so passionately taken to, was bitterly divided about slavery and had entered a civil war.

Beaumont's Memoir of Tocqueville

Three years after Tocqueville's death and already one year into the American Civil War, in 1862, the well-known and respectable Boston publisher Ticknor and Fields brought out a two-volume book entitled *Memoir, Letters, and Remains of Alexis de Tocqueville*.[34] The book, edited and slightly modified to suit the American market, contained not only a long and very personal memoir of Tocqueville by the editor but also hitherto unpublished travel reports, starting with Tocqueville's early travels to Sicily, and observations and notebooks from the trip to America, such as 'Visit to Lake Oneida' and 'A Fortnight into the Wilderness'. Together with excerpts from longer and previously published essays such as 'France before the Revolution' the edition also contained a number of letters which showed a more personal, human and – most important – moral side of Tocqueville's life.

The two-volume book must be considered as an attempt not only to further maintain Tocqueville's reputation as a remarkable observer of American affairs and the author of *Democracy in America* but also at presenting Tocqueville as somebody full of curiosity and, against common perception, as an extremely attractive and morally concerned person. In his memoir of Tocqueville, which introduces the two-volume publication, Beaumont confesses that the task was almost an impossible one: 'We have tried to paint the author, the philosopher, and the statesman; but who can paint the man himself, his heart, his grace, his poetical imagination, and at the same time his good sense'.[35] Beaumont continues:

> Tocqueville not only possessed great talents but every variety of talent. His conversation was as brilliant as his compositions. He was as admirable as a narrator as he was as a writer. He possessed another talent which is even more rare, that of being a good listener as well as a talker ... he found time for everything, and never omitted a moral or a social duty. It has always been said that he had many friends; he had the additional happiness of never losing one ...[36]

This first edition of Tocqueville's unpublished writings and letters is both a declaration of admiration and deep friendship with the deceased and the portrait of a moral man. Man and work are not seen as separate but as one entity.

Beaumont's memoir of Tocqueville, which comprises almost a hundred pages, reads like a draft for a longer and more comprehensive biography, a biography that, as we know now, never materialized. Written in the third person it takes us through the childhood of Tocqueville, his family and upbringing in Paris and the family estate in Normandy, and his early classical studies at a college in Metz. Family influences are also referred to. No less a writer than Malesherbes had been Tocqueville's grandfather. Beaumont noted that Tocqueville had from early on a talent for composition and writing and was at one point awarded a school prize in rhetoric. Travelling and writing about his travels became a passion from early in his life. Beaumont's volume included a longer travel report from 1826 when he visited Sicily, which, although not really comparable to later travel writings, included a remarkable account of the visit to the island. The same is true of his description of Rome. According to Beaumont, these early writings show already a remarkable skill in combining his education in classics with a sense of political decline and tragedy in the case of Rome, something that would later show up in the different contexts of modern historical events. Furthermore these early writing attempts reveal that Tocqueville already paid close attention to institutions and manners.

Beaumont describes how he met Tocqueville as a young *juge auditeur* in Versailles and how he recognized in his friend a genuine capacity for critical judgment and 'a rare faculty of generalization'.[37] These intellectual talents were soon applied to French conditions. Although both Beaumont and Tocqueville came from aristocratic families, they both recognized the massive changes and the new problems that had come about with modern democracy. The great question that the two friends were concerned about were clearly 'How to reconcile equality, which separates and isolates men, with liberty? How to prevent a power, the offspring of democracy, from becoming absolute and tyrannical? ... Was the fate of modern society to be both democracy and despotism?'[38]

Although both friends were thinking alike, Beaumont always saw in Tocqueville a capacity to think further and beyond the surface. There existed in his friend a synthesizing capacity that he saw somewhat lacking in himself. He writes with admiration that Tocqueville was indeed 'a thinker whose brain [was] always at work'.[39] He adds that

> the term thinker would be, however, inappropriate, if applied to him in the ordinary sense of an abstract philosopher who takes pleasure in metaphysical speculations ... such was not Tocqueville, whose speculations had always a practical and definite object. In fact he was little versed in mental science. He had not much taste for it; he was imperfectly acquainted with its language ... its controversies always seemed to him more or less barren ...[40]

Tocqueville always doubted 'the truth', he was truly a thinker in the skeptical tradition. Part of his theoretical-conceptual toolbox were historical experiences and comparison: 'He considered the past only as it affected the present, and foreign countries only with a view to his own'.[41] A clear sign of this skeptical attitude was reflected in his reluctance to welcome the July Revolution of 1830. He saw it as little more than a historical necessity, and after a few months he decided that time and intellectual resources were better spent in observing another society that had emerged from revolutionary struggle – without any terror but with, so it seemed even at the time, lasting functioning institutions.

Beaumont confirmed that the prison project and the joint study that resulted from their visit were only the pretense for having the opportunity to spend nine months in the U.S. studying its institutions and morals. During their visit Beaumont became aware of his friend's peculiar form of note-taking. For Tocqueville nothing ever seemed lost, every bit of information was helpful. Through Beaumont we know that Tocqueville's notebooks served as the basic framework for *Democracy in America*.

Also noteworthy were the numerous conversations between Beaumont and Tocqueville; both used each other as a sounding board for ideas. Over the course of their joint travels they also came to agree on a division of labour. Tocqueville was to work on the 'big comparative issues' and was looking at the big 'drifts' or tendencies of modern society. In contrast, Beaumont was more inclined towards literature and dealing with the underprivileged, the often unpleasant minutiae of the emerging democracy, be they Indians, Black people, women or Irishmen.[42] For this Beaumont found plenty of support from Tocqueville. The same could also be said the other way around: starting with their joint travels they would in the future discuss every page and paragraph they were to publish, what was to be included and what was not. For example, in his attempt to appear more analytical Tocqueville even went so far as not to include his travel reflections in his *Democracy* book as first intended. In the *Memoirs, Letters, and Remains*, however, Beaumont decided to pay homage to the romantic side of Tocqueville and publish two remarkable pieces. They show another side of Tocqueville that few had known before.

On their return to France Tocqueville spent what Beaumont suspects were his happiest years, writing the first volume of *Democracy*. As somebody from an aristocratic background Beaumont judged Tocqueville to have been the ideal person to write a book about democracy. Tocqueville, so he argued, would get the correct balance between striving for equality and the defense of liberty: 'Born in the ranks of the aristocracy, but with a love for liberty, Tocqueville had found modern society in the hands of democracy; and, considering this to be an established fact, which it was no longer possible to question, he thought that to the absolute equality thus produced it was essential to add liberty; for without liberty equality has no check to its impulses, no counterpoise to its oppressions'.[43]

In his portrait Beaumont pays not only homage to Tocqueville the writer and skeptical thinker, he also points to Tocqueville the politician. Being a politician one needs first and foremost a constituency and Tocqueville was lucky to find a base in the old family estate near Cherbourg. But Beaumont stresses also that his friend was too honest, too sincere and perhaps even too sensitive a person to succeed in the political jungle that was the political regime at the time. Furthermore, Beaumont alerts the reader to the possibility that somebody who is a good writer is not necessarily a good public speaker. Far too often one has to cater to the lowest common denominator and that was surely not what Tocqueville wanted – at least not according to Beaumont. This might explain why Tocqueville enjoyed much more working behind the scenes, be it in commissions that dealt with the abolition of slavery or the colonial situation in Algeria. As the statesman that he would become at a later stage – after 1848 Tocqueville was appointed as France's foreign minister – he was much freer from the immediate demands of his constituency and it is here that his two greatest qualities would come to bear: 'first, the glance which penetrates the future; discovers beforehand the path to be followed, the rocks to be avoided ... secondly, a knowledge of men'.[44]

According to Beaumont's account, Tocqueville's hopes were not fulfilled. After the coup of Louis Bonaparte, Tocqueville opted for retirement from politics and returned to writing. His main project was to be a study of the long-term effects of the French Revolution. Like *Democracy*, the study on France was based on historical comparison. This time it was not only the United Kingdom that mattered as a point of reference but Germany as well. While the first part of Tocqueville's book was published, the second remained a torso, fragments of which Beaumont included in the American two-volume collection *Memoir, Letters, and Remains of Alexis de Tocqueville*. Another important manuscript, not included in the edited American collection but referred to in Beaumont's biographical sketch was Tocqueville's *Souvenirs*, a critical reflection of what it meant to be a politician in revolutionary times and, more specifically, what had gone wrong with the attempt to establish the Second Republic.

The biggest praise, however, Beaumont reserved for Tocqueville the letter writer. It is here that we gain a better picture of Tocqueville, the friend, husband and thinker. 'A letter', writes Beaumont, 'is much less an intellectual exercise than an ebullition of feeling, a token of friendship, a passage in one's life, a conversation in which both the heart and the mind take part. A letter is not a study, but a part of the writer's personality that survives it, and prolongs its existence'.[45] Beaumont knew what he was talking about since the two friends exchanged more than 300 letters. It is in Tocqueville's letters that 'he will be known and loved as a man'. 'They will,' Beaumont adds, 'exhibit the author in a new light; for Tocqueville excelled as a letter writer'.[46]

Conclusion

Beaumont, the editor of Tocqueville, has often been criticized for censoring or leaving out certain passages of letters or diaries. Yet without his editorial work we would know very little about the other side of Tocqueville, and we would certainly not know how Tocqueville became 'Tocqueville', democracy's pragmatic prophet we have come to admire so much. Furthermore, the criticism of Beaumont as somebody who only by today's advanced standards failed in his editorial task is not only somewhat ahistorical but also obliterates the enormous motivation, will and sense of duty that drove the man. In contrast to easy retrospective criticism, it seems to me that we can witness in the efforts of Beaumont a fascinating example of nineteenth-century performativity and morally inspired icon-construction, which in turn relied on the conduct and exemplary life of his friend Tocqueville. Beaumont succeeded perhaps less in terms of the standards of critical editorial craftsmanship as they are known today but more in his attempt to serve the long-term reputation and remembrance of his friend.

In terms of Bartmanski and Alexander's criteria alluded to at the beginning of this paper, it becomes obvious that they all apply to our case study: Tocqueville scores highly in terms of liminal time; furthermore he developed charismatic qualities through moral competence; and he identified a set of questions that kept and will continue to keep entire social science departments busy for the foreseeable future. However, as we have also seen, Tocqueville's iconic status is not limited to these criteria but involves very much an active part, with Beaumont at the helm.

Beaumont's performance achieved what it set out to achieve. Having spent considerable time at Tocqueville's deathbed, he could not but realize that Tocqueville was not superhuman. That realization spurred Beaumont on even more, and in the end he discovered not just the meaning of one life (Tocqueville's) but the meaning of two lives (Tocqueville's and his own, by and through intense association and friendship). What Beaumont has done is to construct an iconic figure (Tocqueville) through 'symbolic condensation', just as Alexander has pointed out in his essay on iconic consciousness that I referred to in my introductory remarks. Beaumont shows us Tocqueville as a charismatic figure and theorist whose work we can literally 'sense'. Against Alexander I would call it both an 'experience' *and* a successful communication. Based on the experience of Tocqueville's last days in Cannes, Beaumont shows his friend's life, work and death as that of a human and moral being, not some Nietzschean superhuman being. In other words, Beaumont allows us nothing less than to tap into the moral mind of a charismatic and iconic thinker.

We know from other historical evidence that not all intellectual friendship or attraction turns out like that. Boswell, for example, found his master in Hume and was devastated by Hume's reluctance to go for double insurance by repenting and becoming a believer on the deathbed. What makes the relationship between Beaumont and Tocqueville so unique is that even iconicity and reputation building, which more often than not are accompanied by signs of fierce competition, seem to have left no major injuries. This doesn't happen very often, particularly not in the republic of knowledge. In Beaumont and Tocqueville's case the struggle for intellectual recognition turned both of them into good moral citizens. This is no mean achievement.

---

[1] Dominik Bartmanski, 'How to Become an Iconic Social Thinker: The Intellectual Pursuits of Malinowski and Foucault', in *European Journal of Social Theory*, Vol 15/4 (2012), 427-453: 431f.
[2] Jeffrey C. Alexander, 'Iconic consciousness: the Material Feeling of Meaning', in *Environment and Planning*, 26 (2008), 782-794: 782.
[3] *Ibid.*
[4] I focus here mainly on English-speaking environment, although the story of Tocqueville as an icon is unthinkable without looking into the history of reputation-building in his own country. It is worthwhile noting in this context that Beaumont was the editor of the first French edition of Tocqueville's *Complete Writings* (1864-1866). The story of the French side of reputation-building and intellectual history, which followed Beaumont's pioneering work, has largely been told already, see, for example, Francoise Mélonio, *Tocqueville and the French* (Charlottesville: University Press of Virginia, 1998); Lucien Jaume, *Tocqueville. The Aristocratic Sources of Liberty* (Princeton, NJ: Princeton University Press, 2013); and Robert Darnton, 'How to Become a Celebrity' (review of Antoine Lilti: Figures publiques: L'Invention de la célébrité, 1750-1850, in *New York Review of Books*, 21 May 2015); hence there is no need to repeat any of this here. We also have a couple of studies that tell the story of the relationship between Tocqueville and Beaumont in relation to their joint journey to America and the work that resulted from that: George Wilson Pierson, *Tocqueville and Beaumont in America* (New York: Oxford University Press, 1938), and more recently *Alexis de Tocqueville and Gustave de Beaumont in America: Their Friendship and Their Travels*, ed. Olivier Zunz (Charlottesville: University Press of Virginia, 2011). How the American perception of Tocqueville developed after Tocqueville's death is discussed in Matthew Mancini, *Alexis de Tocqueville and American Intellectuals* (Lanham, MD: Rowman and Littlefield, 2006). The listed titles are all great studies in their own right but what have so far not been studied in greater detail are the early performative aspects of this icon-making process, something I intend to do in this essay.
[5] Alexis de Tocqueville, *Correspondance d'Alexis de Tocqueville et de Gustave de Beaumont, Oeuvres Completes, Tome VIII (3 Vols.)*, ed. J.-P. Mayer (Paris: Gallimard, 1967). See also Alexis de Tocqueville, *Lettres choisies. Souvenirs*, eds. Francoise Mélonio and Laurence Guellec (Paris: Gallimard, 2003).
[6] *Memoir, Letters, and Remains of Alexis de Tocqueville*, ed. Gustave de Beaumont (Boston: Ticknor and Fields, 1862).

7 Between 12 March and 16 April 1859 Beaumont sent 26 letters from Cannes. The letters and their copyright are held by Yale University, Beinecke Rare Book and Manuscript Library (Yale Tocqueville Manuscripts, MS Vault Tocqueville, Section D. IV. r). The letters which I draw upon on the following pages were translated into English by Juliet O'Brien. The translation was funded by University College Dublin's Seed Funding initiative.

8 Beaumont prepared the French edition immediately after Tocqueville's death, which included a memoir of Tocqueville (written by Beaumont), excerpts from Tocqueville's unfinished book on the Revolution in France, some of the more personal essays and a significant numbers of his letters. The American edition (1862) contains some additional fifty-five pages of material that was not contained in the French edition. As to who the editor of that American edition was remains a mystery. While it is certain that Beaumont initiated the American edition and that the book was based on the French edition that he was preparing, he was neither the executive editor nor the translator. Both remained unnamed. For the main argument that is presented here this is of no great significance. As to the details of the 1862 Boston edition see Mancini 2006, 120ff.

9 Letter of Gustave de Beaumont to his wife Clémentine; Paris, 19 January 1859; underlining in the original.

10 Gustave de Beaumont to his wife Clémentine; Paris, 21 January 1859; underlining in the original.

11 At that time Alexis' second brother, Louis-Eduard de Tocqueville was unable to come to Cannes.

12 According to Hugh Brogan's biography *Alexis de Tocqueville* (London: Profile, 2006), 619ff, Tocqueville discussed religion with the two nuns at his bedside. The discussion of religion and belief seemed so unlike the Tocqueville in his prime. Tocqueville, who had always acknowledged the functional aspects of religion for civil society, had never been a great believer. He had always been more of a skeptic in the classical sense of the word. Tocqueville may have sought some confidence or reassurance in the light of his grave illness and, perhaps, the great unknown. Interestingly, Brogan (*ibid*.) refers to an incident where the local priest had been called in to see Tocqueville, yet the latter was reluctant to engage in conversation on the day of the priest's visit, something the two nuns obviously did not like.

13 Gustave and his wife had to deal with an inheritance that left them in debt and made a continuing presence at the estate necessary, a situation which explains the largely silent years of Beaumont's later life.

14 Gustave de Beaumont to his wife Clémentine; Cannes, 12 March 1859.

15 *Ibid*.

16 Gustave de Beaumont to his wife Clémentine; Cannes, 14 March 1859.

17 *Ibid*.

18 Gustave de Beaumont to his wife Clémentine; Cannes, 16 March 1859. Beaumont even points out what a great experience and opportunity it would be for any young intelligent mind to work as a secretary-cum-doctor with the great Tocqueville for a year or even more (*ibid*).

19 *Ibid*., emphasis in the original.

20 Gustave de Beaumont to his wife Clémentine; Cannes, 17 March 1859.

21 *Ibid*., emphasis in the original.

22 Gustave de Beaumont to his wife Clémentine; Cannes, 19 March 1859.

23 Gustave de Beaumont to his wife Clémentine; Cannes, 21 March 1859.

24 *Ibid*.

25 Gustave de Beaumont to his wife Clémentine; Cannes, 23 March 1859.

26 Gustave de Beaumont to his wife Clémentine; Cannes, 27 March 1859.

[27] Gustave de Beaumont to his wife Clémentine; Cannes, 30 March 1859.
[28] *Ibid.*, emphasis in the original.
[29] Gustave de Beaumont to his wife Clémentine; Cannes, 4 April 1859.
[30] *Ibid.*, emphasis in the original.
[31] Gustave de Beaumont to his wife Clémentine; Cannes, 30 March 1859.
[32] Beaumont to his wife Clémentine; Paris, 7 April 1859. Beaumont knew that his friend had always been a person 'disturbed by doubt'. At the same time he knew that Tocqueville's death would be 'that of a Christian, as had been all his life. Conversion has been wrongly spoken of. He had no need for conversion, because he had never been in the slightest degree irreligious ... there could be no liberty without morality, and no morality without religion. Christianity and civilization were to him convertible terms' (*Memoir, Letters and Remains of Alexis de Tocqueville*, 101).
[33] Beaumont to his wife Clémentine; Paris, 16 April 1859.
[34] Alexis de Tocqueville, *Memoir, Letters, and Remains of Alexis de Tocqueville*.
[35] *Ibid.*, 102.
[36] *Ibid.*, 103.
[37] *Ibid.*, 16.
[38] *Ibid.*, 19f.
[39] *Ibid.*, 20.
[40] *Ibid.*
[41] *Ibid.*, 21.
[42] In his own publications Beaumont addressed the question of slaves, Indians and women in his novel-cum-sociological analysis *Marie or Slavery in the United States* (Baltimore: Johns Hopkins University Press, [1835] 1999) and in his book *Ireland: Social, Political and Religious* (Cambridge, MA: Belknap Press of Harvard University Press, [1839] 2006).
[43] *Memoir, Letters, and Remains of Alexis de Tocqueville*, 42.
[44] *Ibid.*, 60.
[45] *Ibid.*, 84.
[46] *Ibid.*, 85.

5 | Philosophical Reflections on Reality and Death – from Plato to Novalis, Schopenhauer, and Pieper

Dan Farrelly

> ... they say Thales[1] was studying the stars, Theodorus, and gazing aloft, when he fell into a well; and a witty and amusing Thracian servant-girl made fun of him because, she said, he was wild to know about what was up in the sky but failed to see what was in front of him and under his feet. The same joke applies to all who spend their lives in philosophy ... The question he asks is, What is man? What actions and passions properly belong to human nature and distinguish it from all other beings? This is what he wants to know and concerns himself to investigate.[2]

In his *Was heisst akademisch?* Josef Pieper (1904-1997) refers to this passage from Plato's *Theaetetus* to highlight the fact that the true philosopher (not necessarily the professional one) concerns himself with knowledge in a way which seems strange to most people – even laughable to some. It is the same feeling of strangeness which would arise in the minds of most people at being asked to take seriously questions that arise from metaphysics, the science of being – being as such. There are very few situations where such a challenge arises – apart, possibly, from some traditionally oriented philosophy courses in universities, where students may be experiencing an introduction to the history of philosophy. It could happen, and almost certainly does sometimes happen, that the study of metaphysical questions is, for a large proportion of students, a mostly cerebral process.

But when does a question of this kind assume 'existential' proportions as opposed to remaining a mainly cerebral function? Possibly, with the experience of a life-threatening illness in one's own life. It could be that, while attending the funeral of a close friend or relative, one asks 'What is death?' In a different context, say for a student of medicine, a rather detached question might be about the physical disintegration of the body. But the real question most likely to concern us in the situations mentioned is, in the words of Alfred North: 'What's it all about?' This is a blunt way of asking the metaphysical question about the meaning of existence – the meaning of an individual person's existence, as well as the meaning of existence as such. What does it mean *to be*? What is *being*?

These questions may not find a satisfactory, clear answer, but they are no laughing matter, and the person who asks them is not the idiot the Thracian servant-girl (and those like her) take him/her to be.

Naturally, it is clear that we are all surrounded by *beings* – persons and things. Then there is the whole *world of being* – the totality at large: the vast areas of our own immediate surroundings; then the aspects of the concrete world we experience daily; the areas we know about from experience of travel; the spheres, the other planets and cosmoi being investigated and studied by physicists. In a sense, all of this is for us individuals a kind of global experience with all the limitations this suggests. We are aware of these vistas, but in what sense do we know them?

For Plato our knowledge of the world is not 'real'. We know only the shadows of reality. We have no direct knowledge of reality as it is in itself. In philosophy in the modern period – roughly since the era of Kant – the same problem has been posed: Can we get behind the so-called world of appearances to know reality as it is in itself? We seem to be looking at something veiled. For most of our time we are content to look at this veil, to live, as we must, in this world of appearances – without reflecting at all on the possibility that it really is merely a world of appearances. Even when we are overcome by wonder at a magnificent view of the sea or the mountains; or at the sight of a new-born child in its mother's arms; or at the sound of an inspired musical creation or other great work of art – if asked what this means, we might well be satisfied to give the facile answer: It is what it is. But this seems to be merely an attempt to avoid searching for an explanation of the experience – perhaps in despair of ever finding a satisfactory answer. What is death? – It is what it is. Does this amount to saying that there is nothing behind the veil of appearances? There is only the veil?

Arthur Schopenhauer, whose work is seen as ground-breaking in the initiation and development of modern existentialism, was a profound admirer of both Plato and Kant. In his monumental work *Die Welt als Wille und Vorstellung* (The World as Will and Representation) Schopenhauer tackles the question of our own individual access to fundamental reality. Fundamental reality is the Will, which is engaged in all aspects of organic and inorganic being. The world as we know it, in all its aspects – personal and otherwise – is no more real for us than it was for Plato or Kant, and no more knowable for what it is. In Schopenhauer's philosophy it is all accounted for as the Will's representation. All our knowing processes get no further than these representations. But, for Schopenhauer, we don't *know* reality intellectually. Instead, we grasp it within ourselves where we experience our own *will* – with its fundamental blind striving, as seen in all of our drives. Our will, the experience of desire in its many facets, is our participation in ultimate reality. We don't 'know' reality, but we live it deep within ourselves. This is the *existential* grasp of reality. The real is experienced in one's own inner life. It is not 'known' (and is therefore not 'representation'), but it is *lived*.

It is fascinating that Pieper, who is no Schopenhauerian, is also convinced that we can have a grasp of profound reality within ourselves: We can become aware of our own individual being – not only in the stark loneliness of our individuality, but also in our limited position in the context of the greater totality of beings and of being as such. For Pieper, the real philosopher – again, not necessarily the professional one! – is the person who lives primarily steeped in and directed by the contemplation of this totality and in the awareness of one's own limited position in it.

The experience of being is seen by Pieper as two-sided: he writes of the *mirandum* – the aspects of reality which inspire in us a sense of wonder: breath-taking admiration for what confronts us in the cosmos, in nature, personal love, music. This kind of experience, this *mirandum*, we feel, takes us beyond ourselves – as it were into another world. In a recent conversation, almost in passing, I experienced an unexpected witness to the reality of this *mirandum*. A plasterer was chatting with me about the bright autumn weather and, without any input from me, he said how he had recently looked up at the clear blue sky and had reflected that it was merely a distant curtain, beyond which there were vast worlds billions of miles away from our world. He referred to photos sent back from 'Voyager I' which show this great earth of ours as the tiniest speck in the universe. No expertise on his part or mine, but it is an example of experiencing the *mirandum*. His curtain, it is true, is still only a physical curtain behind which there is further *physical* reality. With science, that particular curtain disappears, but the veil beyond which we search for *meta*physical reality still exists and philosophers will continue to try to lift it.

But there is also the negative side to the *mirandum*. Wherever we encounter it, it can overpower us. Awareness of the enormous expanse of the sea, of the vast reaches of our cosmos and of the wider universe can have the effect of making us feel dwarfed, totally insignificant. A tiny atom amongst the billions of billions of atoms. The Thracian servant-girl might laugh at someone who expressed such concerns, although, in another way, she is taught the lesson of her own 'insignificance' every day – in the way she is made to 'feel her place', for instance – and the keen eye of the psychologist might observe the various manifestations of her profoundly rooted insecurities. The psychologist, given the opportunity, might look into the family relationships and early childhood experiences of the girl in an attempt to help her to understand the basis of her insecurities.

But for Pieper, the psychologist can only go so far – and not far enough into the person's inner self as to reach the real core of the self. His experience of the shortcomings, for instance of psychotherapy, is expressed in volume 3 of his Autobiography:

> With regard to psychotherapy, I found – as someone necessarily looking in from the outside – confirmation of what I already

knew 'theoretically'. I now became convinced that someone who has such direct access to the methodically exposed central core of another person must himself be 'right' in his thinking about the fundamentals of our existence, and even be 'right' in himself, if incurable damage is to be avoided. But in this case I was not simply an observer. I was involved. Before the treatment began it was carefully explained to me that the son's relationship with the father, which was very close, and perhaps even too close, would probably be dissolved and possibly turn into antagonism. I was prepared for this, and also willing to accept it. But I could not see why this change should be deliberately brought about and, through arbitrary misinterpretation of 'early childhood experiences', should lead not only to his complete alienation but even to his opposition to me, his father, and to all I stood for. This was painful for my son and probably disturbed him even further.[3]

Pieper would insist that the *metaphysical* investigation probes further – into the person's relationship with being as such. Even if the immediate psychological insecurities could be banished by the realization – and perhaps even acceptance – of the elements which caused them; even if this level of insecurity could be overcome, perhaps once and for all, there is still one fundamental insecurity which can never be fully overcome: and that is the worry about what happens to the person at the moment of dying.

Vision and Privileged Moments

In our experience of the *mirandum*, for a moment we perhaps see things differently, more deeply than in our ordinary day-to-day living. There are privileged moments where, with Goethe's Faust we might be tempted to say, 'Verweile doch, du bist so schön!' ['Stay a while. You are so beautiful'.] But we know that the moment is fleeting, and the 'ordinary' returns. The work of the great Romantic poet, Novalis, reflects his belief in – experience of? – the interpenetration of two worlds: the day-to-day, and the other world. Awareness of the other world is, for Novalis, not just to be had in dreams or in the imagination. It is, at the very least, a recurring experience, so that it is possible to live with this relatively constant experience. In this context, death is seen as the gentle transition to the other world, which, even as we live, preoccupies us, at least in privileged moments. Death merely dissolves the bonds that tie us to the ordinary world we know.

Metaphysics is focused on being as such and on being in its concrete manifestations. In one sense, it is the most abstract of all types of knowledge. It offers nothing to our senses – we can neither see it, nor hear it, nor feel it nor even imagine it. It is not 'this' or 'that' but simply everything. What is particularly striking in Pieper's work is that he identifies the *mirandum* as being itself. The privileged moment is the awareness – which defies adequate formulation – of being confronted with being as such.

It is not unusual for us to call things 'amazing', 'wonderful', 'incredible'. Nelson Mandela is 'a legend'. These are ordinary terms we use for things, performances, people we admire. The terms themselves become impoverished clichés. They are used all the time, normally reflecting the fact that we are lost for words. Sometimes, our admiration of, say, a concert performance or a dramatic scene in a play is expressed first in a deep silence within ourselves before – and after – we join in the applause. If someone says, 'That was amazing', our answer – if we agree – might well be, 'Yes, incredible'. This fundamental 'speechlessness', could well be followed by analytic speech in which we break down the elements which obviously contribute to the performance: the clear diction, the phrasing, the breath control, the purity of sound, the presence, the passion, the star quality etc. But in such analysis we are aware that with our words we are 'dissecting' something without really accounting for the life that was in it. The *mirandum* is beyond our words. But it is nonetheless real for us.

With regard to Novalis, it is worth remembering that he was not a dreamy artist but a scientist engaged in mining. As is clear from his *Hymns to the Night,* he had, like many a contemporary scientist, studied the findings of astronomers and was aware of the vast expanses of our universe and beyond. In the case of Novalis, naivety is out of the question. He was fascinated by the sources of light and the vast dimensions of the universe from which it originates. But for Novalis there is a still more important dimension to life. In his work in mining, he spends time under the earth – in the inside of things. 'Wir träumen von Reisen durch das Weltall – ist denn das Weltall nicht in uns? Nach innen geht der geheimnisvolle Weg'. [We dream of journeys through the cosmos – is the cosmos, then, not within us? The mysterious path leads inwards.] Within the self, in one's own conscious life, one finds fundamental meaning. As with Plato, Kant, and Schopenhauer there is, for Novalis, an exterior world in which he lives and an inner world where ultimate meaning is to be found.

If we limit the comparison here to Schopenhauer and Novalis, the former finds ultimate reality at work in the human will, which he sees as the focus of the Will as opposed to the world of representations. Only within the function of one's own will is it possible to experience ultimate reality. Contemplation of the world of representations is fruitless unless it points us – as through profound experience of music, for example – to the centre within us to which it speaks. The inner self referred to here is not that examined by the psychologists, which relates to our external experience and interprets its effects on us, but the metaphysical self, which lies far deeper, beyond the concrete realm. [I hear the peals of laughter coming from the Thracian maid!]

The whole question is whether there *is* a metaphysical self directly accounted for by a creative force which it is impossible to define but which seems to impinge on our lives, leading us sometimes to suspect that a particular pattern has been given to our lives, with a shape and ongoing continuity in a particular direction.

This sort of experience was known to Novalis in his personal life. His love of his fiancée Sophie continued after her early death. As the *Hymns to the Night* and his *Heinrich von Ofterdingen* novel show, he remained preoccupied with this love. At her graveside he experienced a conversion from the world of light to the world of death, and while continuing to function fruitfully in the world of light he became aware of the interpenetration of the two spheres, so that, in a sense, he was already dead as he continued to live.

The *Titanic*

In 1912, the *Titanic* was the greatest modern ship of its time. Constructed in Belfast by Harland and Wolff in an enterprise combining the most advanced technical skills with enormous capital investment and exploiting the working poor of Belfast and surrounding shipbuilding areas in Britain – the unprotected scaffolding of the gantry, combined with long hours and hunger contributing to the death of one building worker per day – this giant ship soon suffered a sobering tragedy. Stretching more than 250 metres in length across the surface of the Atlantic, the ship had its metal sides disturbed in its lateral collision with an iceberg. For over two hours it took in water and then plunged perpendicularly to its 'death' on the bottom of the Atlantic to a depth of two and a half miles. In terrifying irony and in a stark image of our minute importance in the context of the universe, the greatness of the *Titanic* was soon dwarfed by the enormity of the ocean.

This image of the great product, like a mighty plank, disappearing entirely out of sight at great speed in a perpendicular downward thrust, could be interpreted as a symbol representing the negation of man's pride in his achievements. But it need not be used, negatively, as a striking example of the futility of human endeavour. Yet it does, above all, point to the fact that, unexpectedly, the 'unsinkable' can sink. It also raises the question: What then? Most immediately, there was the comforting of the survivors and mourning for the dead; and the inevitable attempts to account for the sinking – the shifting of the steel plates on the side of the ship, the inferior material of the rivets used in certain parts of the ship's sides. But the philosophical question does not concern what mistakes were made. Such questions could be answered in time. The question that concerns us, as individuals – should we choose to entertain it – is whether that was really the end of the people who drowned or whether their *being* survives in a meaningful form, and as what. The philosopher, Josef Pieper, admits that no clear, satisfactory answer can be given to this ultimate question, but he also says that that is not a reason to cease asking it. Various aspects of our experience, the ones that encourage us to wonder and to hope, need to be explored. It is impossible for us to see into the way the victims of the *Titanic* debacle handled their confrontation with death. Did they accept death, in faith, as from the hand of God? Did they despair? The same questions can be asked of the multitude of people who die from natural disasters and from barbaric military actions that destroy scores of people at a time. Our helplessness in the face of these questions throws us back on our own subjective experience where it prompts us to affirm our involvement in another dimension, another world into which we sense the possibility of a transition. We may side with those who are convinced that, while living what is seen as our ordinary lives, we transcend these lives by living in the awareness of another dimension. Various experiences make us wonder, so that we brave the ridicule of the 'Thracian maid' and her many allies, and leave room in our lives for the transcendent.

The Death of Socrates

In Plato's dialogue on the death of Socrates there is direct confrontation with the experience of dying and an attempt to analyse what can be said about the afterlife. Josef Pieper, whose own philosophical work is rooted in Plato's philosophy, published a book of three plays for television, the third of them entitled *The Death of Socrates*. In this third play the action takes place in the death cell, where Socrates is condemned to drink a cup of poison. It is the execution of his death sentence, a punishment for arousing the wrath and enmity of many leading citizens of Athens by proving to them that they are fundamentally ignorant. He claims that they know nothing and he has continually striven to prove it to them. He claims to know nothing himself – the difference between them and him being that they *think* they have knowledge of reality, and in fact don't have it; whereas he, while not having knowledge of reality, also does not think he has!

In this play, as in the others in the book, there is often reference to 'the many' – 'hoi polloi'. The term is not used in any superior, contemptuous tone, but refers to the standpoint of most people – like its representative, the Thracian serving girl – the many. When we are confronted with a major catastrophe like the sinking of the *Titanic* – or the more cataclysmic ones like the slaughter of millions in the world wars and modern genocides – our most obvious reaction is probably shock at the extent of the human devastation involved. Our humanity is touched by these events and by many catastrophes occurring frequently but on a much smaller scale. The 'polloi' are profoundly affected by such things and respond with generosity in their endeavours to alleviate the sufferings of survivors.

Naturally, we cannot know to what extent those most associated with such cataclysmic experiences are led to pose questions about the fundamental meaning of life – when so many lives are absurdly obliterated. If they ask, 'What does it all mean?' they might answer: 'Nothing! It is meaningless!' Or, with Socrates, they might say: 'I don't know!'

Faced directly with his own imminent death, this self-confessed 'agnostic' has his own grip on reality. The exposition of his point of view comes most clearly into focus not in the context of abstract philosophical discussion but at the point where the pressing question arises of his escape from the prison and from death. His influential, pragmatic friend Crito, who had already given his personal guarantee to the court that Socrates would not abscond, has nevertheless bribed the jailor and has laid plans for Socrates's escape. Crito, along with Socrates's circle of friends who are gathered in the prison, is astonished when Socrates refuses to escape from the influence of the law. Socrates is party to a contract, and his commitment to truth forbids him to break the contract. There is such a thing as truth and right. Not that truth is definable in any set of propositions, no more than right can be determined once and for all by any set of laws. But when we are true we are aware of it, just as, when we are not true, we are aware of that also. Similarly, when we do right we are aware of it, and when we do wrong we are aware of it. This is not the knowledge of 'philosophers'; it is our fundamental awareness of reality. To act against what we know is true and right would define us in a way that would have consequences for us in our death. As Socrates says, we take nothing with us into death but what we are.

In the context of discussing what happens to us after death, Socrates at first seems to fall back on Greek mythological images of the dead being taken into another world – where there is reward for the good, purification for the less good, and eternal punishment for the evil. As he spells out the details of the various fates – dwelling with the gods as reward; a kind of purgatory as a means of purification; a hell from which there is no escape – we recognize the clear affinity with the Christian imagery. When one of his circle, Simmias, says: 'So you yourself consider that this is only a story?' Socrates replies:

> No, not 'only' a story! A story, yes. Symbolic speech, an allegory, an image. But this image is completely true! In all of our investigations we will find nothing of greater truth. – And

that this fits more or less with the way it will be with our souls and their dwelling place – that is something we should surely dare to believe. ... In any case, a person who during his lifetime is concerned to embellish his soul not with external things but with things proper to himself: with truth, justice, bravery – such a one has nothing to fear. He can face the journey into Hades and be ready to go when the time comes.

The stark and radical nature of this stance is reflected in the philosopher's response to Crito's question:

Do you have any tasks for those of us here, for me or for the others? For instance, with regard to your sons? – Or is there anything else we could do for you? *Socrates looks at him very calmly. The tone of his answer is indulgent and unwavering.* Nothing else, Crito, except what I have always been speaking about. Care for yourselves in the proper way – that is how you will be doing the best for me and yourselves, and also for my loved ones. ... But if you lose sight of what is truly good for you ... you could promise me as much as you like, and then ...[4]

---

[1] Thales was the first founder of Greek natural philosophy, sixth century B.C.
[2] Translated as *What Does Academic Mean?* by Dan Farrelly (South Bend: St Augustine's Press, 2015), 10.
[3] Josef Pieper, *Eine Geschichte wie ein Strahl. Autobiographische Aufzeichnungen seit 1964* (Munich: Kösel Verlag, 1988), 15f. To appear with St Augustine's Press in 2017 in an English translation by Dan and Una Farrelly.
[4] Josef Pieper, *Kümmert Euch Nicht um Sokrates (*Kösel-Verlag München, 1988), 189. The English translation by Dan Farrelly will be published by St. Augustine's Press in 2017.

6 | Human Attitudes towards the Death of Animals

Alan Baird

'Nor dread nor hope attend a dying animal'. These lines of the poet Yeats open the Introduction of the previous volume in this series *Dublin Death Studies*. Such an anthropocentric statement may be accounted for by Yeats being 'much more a product of urban English culture than of rural Irish culture.'[1] Rurality therefore contributes not only to societal attitudes to death but also to the interactions and relationships people have with animals. Animals die and humans are just another species. At a molecular and cellular level there are more features in common than different between mammals and most living things. Life itself is an organized transient reversal of universal entropy. Chemically and physically the processes of life are broadly understood. The beautiful spiral of nucleic acids upon which all the other polymers of life depend is still a recent discovery and the technological and conceptual revolution which it has spawned is currently under way. However much light has already been shed on ontogeny; development patterns of embryos are common to all mammals. Canonical prototype gene sequences and biochemical pathways are quite highly conserved across plant and animal kingdoms yet we persist in concentrating on differences between species rather than aspects which are common or shared. Are humans so distinct?

In this brief essay the basis of human and non-human animal relationships will be summarized as a platform for actual and literary considerations of the implications of death, burial and the afterlife for non-human mammals. For a more extensive narrative, Spellman's recent book *A Brief History of Death*[2] is very readable. Human attitudes to, and relationships with, other species are complex.

> No one, I presume, doubts that the large proportion which the size of man's brain bears to his body, compared to the same proportion in the gorilla or orang, is closely connected with his mental powers.
>
> Charles Darwin[3]

The view that humanity is just another species is one that may be uncomfortable for some. But then hubris is presumably a human-specific trait. For expediency, the subject matter is restricted to the five or so per cent of animal species (mostly mammals) to which aretaic values have been ascribed.

Historical Context

What distinguishes human beings (specifically *Homo sapiens*) from other creatures is the consequence of a sequence of societal revolutions beginning in pre-history, about 70,000 years ago. The first of these, which has been termed the cognitive revolution, covers a period when human species began to migrate and to behave distinctively through communicating not only large quantities of information about their world but also by the capacity to imagine things which do not actually exist. There can be little doubt that it is the size of a human brain which provides the complexity to manage cognitive tasks. Brain development in human embryos takes about a month longer than that of monkeys. Postnatal neuronal development is also protracted in humans compared with other species, taking over 10 years in humans compared with less than four years in monkeys.[4] The process of encephalization by evolution is likely to result from several drivers[5] and may reflect whether humans are separated from other animals through divine design or due to psychological development and altered levels of awareness.

Regardless of its causes, encephalization coincided with the birth of mythology and folklore which in turn led to cooperation and sharing of behaviours among increasingly larger social groups of hominids. At this time, when language was also developing, the capacity to consider and share abstract thoughts also arose. From this, belief systems and religions developed. The relationships between not only *Homo sapiens* and animals, but also other *Homo* species widened, perhaps contributing to, or at least concident with, extinction of neanderthals and other hominid species.

During the next phase shift in human development, the agricultural revolution, the relationship between humans and animals extended beyond one that was primarily based on foraging (hunting and gathering) to one based on herding, domestication and farming. During the development of animal domestication, ownership then as now was associated with wealth. Another feature was the veneration of certain species reflected in evidence of ritualization of animal slaughter.

Animals and Society

From the times of Plato and Aristotle an often religious hierarchical structure of the Universe was postulated. From such anthropological roots philosophers developed and expressed a wide variety of zoocentric themes. Significant contributors include Voltaire, Rousseau, Schopenhauer and Darwin who have espoused philosophies beyond the simple Aristotelian view that the existence of animals was solely to provide for human needs (although Aristotle believed that all living things have souls). Much of the evidence of the developing attitudes of humans to animals is derived from and reflected in imagery through the ages. Kalof has documented a rich archive of material with which she traces human awareness of, and attitudes to, animals with which we share this planet.[6]

One of the first philosophers to engage in a focussed manner with zoocentrism was Jeremy Bentham who is widely credited as the founder of modern utilitarianism. Bentham's views underpinned much of what society now regards as a base from which human-animal relations is discussed. In brief, human attitudes to non-human animals can be summarized by assigning animals to four domains: *friends*, *tools*, *vermin* or *demons*.. A fifth domain, the imaginary animal, is one which is important in literature, mythology and belief systems. Bentham's insight into the fact that differences between species are sometimes eclipsed by their similarities is borne out by modern science.

Prehistoric humans had a reasonably good awareness of animal anatomy and behaviour as evidenced by Paleolithic cave paintings. Presumably the interest here was derived from a need to understand the prey to be hunted, upon which survival of the early humans depended. The human transition from hunting to herding behaviour is reflected in art from the Upper Paleolithic period which indicates that horses were being harnessed. From the same time period bone fragments have been discovered which indicate selective animal breeding (genetic engineering). Thus from about 5000 BC there was animal domestication and ownership associated with wealth. Uses of animals other than tools or sources of food came to include worship of certain species or of gods with zoomorphic appearance.[7] Also at this time, on several continents, there is evidence of ritualization of animal slaughter performed by priests. Only meat from animals killed in a particular manner could be eaten – practices which remain quite common today in several cultures.

During the Middle Ages attitudes to animals was influenced by religion. The thirteenth-century scholar and author of the compendium *De proprietatibus rerum* (*On the Properties of Things*)[8], Bartholomaeus Anglicus wrote that animals had been created for the use of humans. Specifically, deer and cattle were for eating. Beasts of burden such as horses, donkeys, oxen and camels were for helping. The purpose of monkeys, songbirds and peacocks was for amusement and the creation of bears, lions and snakes was to remind humans of the power of God. Also during the Middle Ages as agriculture developed and also in response to plagues, pestilence and famine, human relationships with animals changed.

Medieval animal illustrations are included in the Bestiary manuscripts, richly illuminated works describing the appearance and habits of a large number of familiar and exotic animals, both real and legendary. Characteristics of these beasts are frequently allegorized, with the addition of notions of morality, which were popular throughout Europe, North Africa, and the Middle East at a time when people were increasingly dependent upon domesticated animals. Not all literary depictions of animals in medieval times were religious, though many stories which have survived in popularity retain a moral message such as those of Aesop the slave.

In contrast to the anatomically accurate representations of animals in Neolithic cave paintings, medieval images of animals are often not realistic but imaginary. They include fabulous creatures such as dragons, unicorns, griffins and chimeras. Interestingly, reality is catching up with fiction. Chimeric animals are currently being generated through applications of powerful technologies derived from the biological revolution. Stem cell biology and gene editing techniques are currently enabling the generation of humanized materials as drugs or vaccines. Intact organs such as hearts, kidneys and lungs grown in non-human donor animals can be harvested to replace failing organs in human recipients. In the twenty-first century the chimera is real.

During the Enlightenment (c. late 1600s-1800) animal use as human commodities (tools) continued to develop. As societies became more urban earlier superstitions and beliefs were challenged. Scientific disciplines were reinforced and organized religion began to lose much control over society. At this time, anatomists were permitted to perform autopsies which had previously been forbidden by the church. Animal dissection and experimentation remain prevalent in teaching and research in modern medicine. Vesalius (1514–64) was a teacher of anatomy and physiology who published *Some Observations on the Dissection of Living Animals*[9] in which, through use of vivisection, he informed medical understanding and promoted research. Descartes (1596–1650) hypothesized that animals were incapable of thinking and, since only humans had souls, only humans could reason.[10] The doctrine of Descartes, one of animal automatism, was expressed thus

> Animals ... act naturally and mechanically, like a clock which tells the time better than our judgement does. Doubtless when the swallows come in spring, they operate like clocks ... Their instinct to bury their dead is no stranger than that of dogs and cats which scratch the earth for the purpose of burying their excrement; they hardly ever actually bury it, which shows that they act only by instinct and without thinking.[11]

Such views align with an earlier concept of an hierarchical 'Great Chain of Being' in which plants, animals, humans, and even angels were ranked from low to high.

The morality of using animals as chattels or tools was examined somewhat empirically by Kant (1724–1804) who proposed that people have moral duties regarding the natural world. People who torment animals are likely to do the same to humans. In a twisted way, cruelty towards animals was neither condemned or considered wrong *per se*, but because of its consequences for humans. Kant advocated a rule-based approach or deontology, such that any action is either morally right or wrong. This extended to duties or responsibilities to animals which were a function of their use as 'man's instruments'. Contemporary sociological research has generated evidence which does bear out Kant's hypothesis that people who behave cruelly to animals behave similarly to other people. Animal cruelty leads directly to interpersonal aggression by desensitizing the individual to violence.[12]

Human attitudes to animals

Due to urbanization and the agricultural revolution the move of the bulk of the population away from intimacy with production animals had begun. During the Renaissance the keeping of pets became popular and animal use in circuses, menageries and displays such as bear-baiting and bull-fighting, which had existed as organized entertainment in earlier times, became regarded as an institutionalized form of public theatre. The Great Plague was spread by verminous rats. Deontology was integrated into utilitarianism which may be summarized that it is the outcome which determines the moral worth of an action. In this approach human use of animals is described as moral if it maximizes happiness and minimizes suffering for all those involved, animals included. Bentham's views, which were broadly extended to those on human slavery, underpinned the development of the animal rights movement. While differences between humans and non-human animals were acknowledged their similiarities were also recognized in the context of attitudinal frame shifts. These include the scientific revolution which triggered the industrial revolution, the information revolution and then the biotechnological revolution, which is still wet behind the ears. These revolutions were not precipitous; they occurred over fairly protracted periods of time in order to grow and mature, often with attendant cultural changes. The current view of the World Economic Forum is that we are in a fourth industrial revolution which is a work in progress.[13]

Death

In order to comprehend death as a process, rather than a metaphysical entity or event, it is important to understand life as a process the cessation of which defines death. Life is a series of coordinated, homeostatically regulated conditions which distinguish animals and plants from inorganic matter. It includes the capacity for growth, reproduction, activity, and eventual (inevitable) death. The chemical composition of animals is extraordinarily conserved between species. Although there are phenotypic variations in comparative anatomy, most cellular and organ-level functions are common to most species of fish, birds or mammals. The arrangements of chemicals within living cells, organized into intact organisms with complex circulatory systems is strong evidence of a common basis to life. Modern biology and progress in understanding the molecular basis of life has also delivered insights into mortality and death.

> For what happens to the children of man and what happens to the beasts is the same; as one dies, so dies the other. They all have the same breath, and man has no advantage over the beasts, for all is vanity. All go to one place. All are from the dust, and to dust all return.
>
> Ecclesiastes 3:19-20

Fig. 6.1) The pet cemetery in the grounds of Powerscourt House, Co. Wicklow, Ireland. Courtesy of Powerscourt Estates.

The permanent cessation of the vital functions is also common to all species including humans. Death is a critical component of the process of natural selection by which animals less adapted to their environment are more vulnerable and have a reduced chance of contributing to the future gene pool. Forensic aspects of the processes involved in living as well as in dying are conserved across all animals. Corpses of all living organisms begin to decompose immediately after death. The facts and processes of animal and human death are largely identical, distinct only in societal views and legal aspects. Ceasing to exist is an inevitable consequence of mortality, however that end is achieved. That reality has not changed but human perceptions have.

Death has commonly been considered as a sad or unpleasant occasion, due to bonds of affection to the person or animal who has died (Figs. 6.1 and 6.2). One hundred years ago death was a more normal feature of everyday existence than it is for most people who will read this. Much of the world's population is Western, Educated, Industrialized, Rich and Democratic (W.E.I.R.D.). Consequently they have experienced improvements in public health and reductions in infant mortality. The lack of local wars has further pushed the dying contingent into the older or ill groups of society from which we separate ourselves by hospitals and

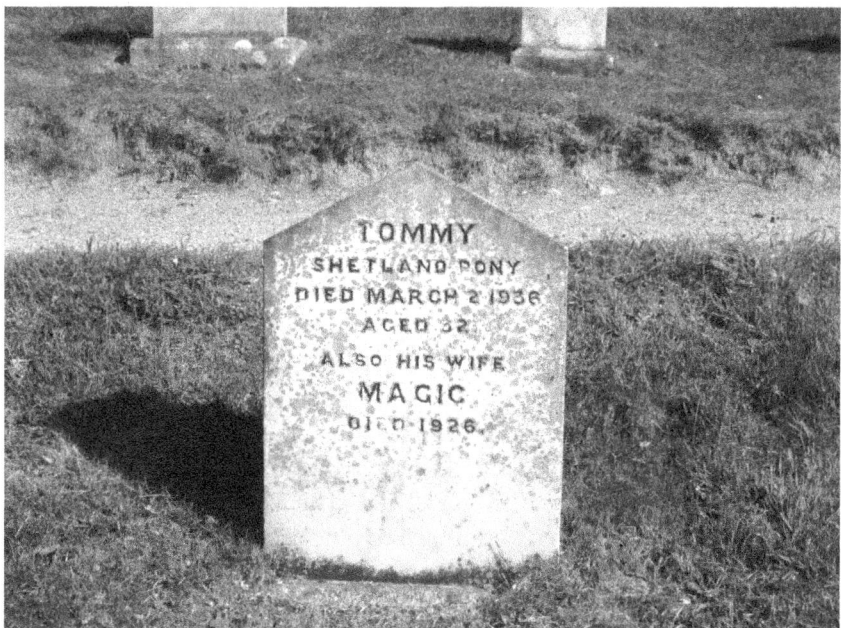

Fig. 6.2) Example of tombstone over pet grave in the pet cemetery in the grounds of Powerscourt House. Courtesy of Powerscourt Estates.

care homes. Thus people are less familiar and perhaps even ill-equipped to deal with death. We often shield children from the rituals of death. Their first encounter with real death may be at the time of loss of a family pet. At such times grieving and coping attitudes are very real and often intense, certainly for children. Animal death has become more significant as human death has become depersonalized.

Very few non-human animals die of old age. Natural causes include predation, disease and trauma or other external hazards to which wild animals succumb. Animals bred for food have death engineered into their routine. In contrast, companion animals such as pets tend to match their owners in terms not only of life-style but also their susceptibilites to disease. Vast numbers of animals are killed by humans. 150 billion animals per year are sacrificed for human use; literally on an industrial scale. According to the statistics of the Farm Animal Rights Movement (FARM), an average North American who eats meat consumes around 30 land animals and an estimated 150-200 aquatic animals each year. Thus over 15,000 individual animals may fuel a three score years and ten lifespan. Smaller but still significant numbers of animals are managed by culling or by euthanasia; about 3 million cats and dogs each year, according to the animal rights organization PETA (People for the Ethical Treatment of Animals). Animals are also killed in time of war or by terrorist actions. This has been dramatized for example in the film *War Horse* and symbolized by the case of Sefton, a horse which survived the Hyde Park bombing in 1982 (which killed four people) and has been recognized as significant in attitudes of the UK public to terrorism.

Killing animals is common practice with a variety of human and societal views which underpin moral and ethical questions and concerns. Ritual slaughter remains not uncommon; a feature which may have its anthropological roots in transition from hunting which has also retained some ritual aspects.[14] Thus killing animals for food (survival, preference or gluttony) or for scientific purposes, including education, are questions for public debate and should be non-taboo issues governed by varying degrees of public understanding and of legislation. Attitudes to animal killing by humans often align to the four sociozoological domains described previously. Eradication of vermin may prevent disease. Demon-killing may reduce real or imagined risk to people or society. Animal 'tools' include food-animals bred for the purpose of being killed. Beasts of burden or performance animals (such as horses and greyhounds), when they are no longer useful for human needs, may be despatched by euthanasia. Companion animals, including guide dogs, occupy a separate domain in terms of how they are not only viewed but treated by humans.

Veterinary healthcare practice has pretty clear attitudes to euthanasia in a context where relief from suffering of a sentient animal is, or should be, a principal driver. In contrast, in human medicine there is much less agreement. The plurality of views regarding animal and human end-of-life matters relates to many general aspects of moral philosophy.

Changing human attitudes to death maps generally to the evolution of human attitudes to animals. Kellehear describes four phases which reflect the social history of dying.[15] These begin with an afterlife journey (beliefs which appeared during the Stone Age). Secondly came the concept of Good Death followed by Managed Death which accompanied the emergence of settlement cultures and cities. Finally, in the modern era Kellehear describes the Shameful Death, when the prospect of death is unclear to people. It is exacerbated when the dying are removed from the family and placed in health care settings where medical attention rather than dying is the priority. This distances the actual experience of dying from the community, leading to an even further reduction in an individual capacity to comprehend it. As we shall see, this gap is partially filled, but not completely met, by the experience of loss of a family pet.

How non-human species have been portrayed in history, art, literature and cinema both reflect and inform human attitudes to death and to themselves. Animal death has been depicted allegorically, satirically and in fables. Seminal examples include 'The Lowest Animal' by Mark Twain.[16] Twain's cynicism appears based on human interactions during religious wars upon which he reflects. He attempts to convince his readers that Darwinian theory of the *Ascent of Man from the Lower Animals* be replaced by a truer one to be named the *Descent of Man from the Higher Animals*. A similar change is outlined in *Death of a Pig,* in which E.B. White describes a complete turnaround in his attitude to an animal which he had initially acquired for its meat. The experience set the scene for his later popular work *Charlotte's Web* which is widely read by children and adults alike.[17]

Anthropomorphic symbolism and examples of death are common in folklore and in literature. They include humanization of animal deaths and bestialization of human death. Few are as stark as the obscenity of dying represented in *Le Grand Troupeau* (translated into English as *To the Slaughterhouse*).[18] In this novel, based on his own experiences of the Great War, Jean Giono graphically describes butchery of animals in a military abbatoir alongside the suffering and dying of wounded soldiers. People are dehumanized as they die 'like animals'. In contrast, the death of Bambi's mother in the Walt Disney cartoon (*Bambi*, 1942) represents humanification of an animal's death. Generations of people have grown up with animated stories contributing to their understanding of the concepts of death and loss. This has become a mainstream phenomenon. According to a study published in the *British Medical Journal* two-thirds of all animated films aimed at children featured the on-screen death of a major character, significantly more so than in films for adults.[19] Yet this has emerged at a period in history in which death has become an increasingly taboo subject for discussion. Adults might instead seek to protect children from the subject of death by using metaphorical language such as speaking of a loved one who has died as 'passed away' or 'gone'. Thus it is left to story-telling and literature, including film to help children develop some level of understanding of death.

Death is inevitable – or is it? The recent and ongoing revolution in science of life has led to challenges of definition. For example, we now have 'immortalized' cell lines which can be maintained in laboratory conditions for as long as their metabolic needs are supplied. Such cell lines, which have even been proposed as a separate species,[20] are routinely employed in vaccine and drug research and development. They have been used to gain a new understanding of fundamental biological processes and have partially replaced animals in scientific research. Human (not donor animal) insulin can be produced, and human-derived stem cells offer replacement tissues and organs; very much part of the fourth industrial revolution. Cloning which is already commercially available for companion animals offers a replacement strategy for failing bodies. Human and animal cadavers lie frozen in cryogenic conditions awaiting resurrection.

Death Rituals

Ritualized slaughter of animals for human consumption is mentioned briefly above. Other rituals are associated with non-human animals – humans are not the only species to bury their dead. Burial of human remains is an established rite for celebrating, respecting, sanctifying, or remembering the life of a person who has died. Burial or interment of animals by members of their own species has been reported. The simple expedient of burial is an effective waste management strategy. It permits recycling of water, organic matter and minerals. Unless protected by encasement or mummification corpses will decompose, mostly due to the action of microbes. Post-mortem changes begin quickly and are progressive. They include the processes of autolysis and putrefraction during which time volatile organic products, including chemicals with exotic names such as putrescine and cadaverine, are produced. These volatile agents are, in part, responsible for the stench of decay. These same chemicals are also signalling molecules via the sense of smell.

Perhaps the evolution of the nastiness of such a sensation is a selected survival characteristic which protects members of a population from eating or even approaching decomposing carrion with its attendant health risks.

More spiritual reasons for burial include respect for mortal remains or an effort to bring closure to grieving. Burial has become an established funeral rite for celebration, sanctification or memorial. As recently as 2013, a newly described hominid species (*Homo naledi*) from over ten million years ago was discovered along with evidence that they intentionally deposited their dead. Thus systematic or organized interment was practiced by early hominids, coinciding with evolving encephalization which underpins high level thinking and social awareness. Rituals and practices around burial have changed from the time of hunter-gatherers through the development of city states along with a developing folklore and mythology which included stories of animal as well as of human burials. Rituals around the process of burial are a feature of many cultures and funerary customs and practices have evolved for both human and animal corpses. Archaeological evidence of animal burials by humans indicates that this is an ancient and widespread practice.[21]

Co-burial of humans and dogs appears to have been quite common practice in ancient Egypt.[22] A 12,000 year old tomb excavated in Israel contained the skeletons of a woman and a young dog.[23] Egyptian culture has famously over many centuries developed elaborate rituals associated with death, burial and the afterlife. Practices include systematically burying animal remains which are often carefully prepared through mummification. The reasons for animals accompanying human interments are not clear but may include aspirations that the recently dead would be joined in the afterlife by their worldly companion(s). Alternatively co-interment may have been to provide offerings to some deity and / or to the deceased to nourish them on the next part of their post-mortem journey.

In ancient Ireland deposition of animal bones that appear to represent offerings was also quite common.[24] Examples cover periods from around 3600 BC in which bones of over fifty cattle were placed in the base of the ditch of an enclosure at Kilshane, Co. Meath. At Ballyeeskeen, Co. Sligo and in Glencurran Cave disarticulated human bones were deposited during the Bronze Age with at least one intact child burial along with new born domesticates (piglets, calves, lambs and hares). At Farta, Co. Galway there is a round barrow covering an Early Bronze Age burial in which were the remains of an adult woman and next to it the skeleton of a seven-year-old stallion.[25]

Two separate industries grew around Egyptian burial practices. The first was to supply people with mummified animals to accompany them into the afterlife. Millions of animals were mummifed and, at least one species, the Sacred Ibis became extinct. Populations of companion animals also dropped significantly since, for example, enormous numbers of cats were used in this way. The scale of a second industry around burial of animals is reflected by the fact that about twenty tons of mummified cats (the average weight of a live adult cat is around 4kg) were exported from Egypt to London in 1890 to be used as agricultural fertilizer. This is in sharp contrast to the care with which ancient Egyptians treated animals which was consistent with a high degree of respect for them whether as companions, food sources or even as as representatives of gods.

Funerary customs which include the complex of beliefs and practices used by a culture to remember the dead have been extensively extended to animals even in modern times. Such practice, which reflects the grief humans harbour for their pets is widespread and, in spite of the fact that there is quite stringent legislation, many urban gardens accommodate the mortal remains of non-human family members. More recently commercial pet cemeteries, funeral services and even dedicated crematoria represent yet more associated industries. In fiction a pet cemetery provided a venue for Waugh's wickedly satirical novel *The Loved One*.[26]

Afterlife

For most non-human animals the afterlife involves being eaten by other animals, including humans – as carrion, as prey or through agriculture or aquaculture. A more mystical view of the afterlife aligns to the concept of death being closely related to one of human nature. In many religions and belief systems the possibility of an afterlife is envisaged. The concept may involve some form of resurrection or an inner soul, which is nonmaterial, or even a physical body. A form of immortality in which identity or consciousness continue after death is a common theme in philosophy, religion, mythology and fiction. Does such an anthropocentric view apply to non-human animals? Perhaps it is recognition or awareness of death that separates humans from creatures which are regarded as sentient but with a less developed level of understanding. Thus the extended concept of life after death may be unique to humans. Pagan and primitive human cultures shared mystic beliefs in animals having souls. Insofar as belief systems are constructs,

> Who knows whether the spirit of man goes upward and the spirit of the beast goes down into the earth?'
> Ecclesiastes 3:21

attitudes emanating from them may and do change as a conseqence of evolution, revolution or revelation.

Since the beginnings of humanity ancient cultures and religions have left behind evidence of belief in an afterlife. For example, almost 4,000 years ago Indians and Egyptians postulated a judgment after death. Many flavours of afterlife have been described.[27] The earliest Hindu texts contain details of funeral rites and the metaphysics of reincarnation. Buddhists maintain that rebirth takes place without an unchanging self or soul passing from one form to another. The type of rebirth will be conditioned by the moral tone of the person's actions (karma). For example, if a person has committed harmful actions in life based on greed, hatred and delusion, rebirth will be in the form of a lower realm, perhaps as an animal.

The concept of soul is contradicted by the most fundamental principles of evolution.[28] However, within many organized religions views relating to whether non-human animals have souls are complex and even ambiguous. Broadly speaking, Christian religions are neither clear nor unclear as to whether animals possess souls. Anglicans and Methodists are generally positive in believing that animals do indeed have souls. In Catholicism, Popes have offered different views of animal afterlife, falling short of doctrinal statements. The theologian Cardinal Newman was very clear on the subject of the soul being restricted to humans alone. In contrast the Orthodox Church, Judaism and Islam appear to share the general belief that animals possess souls. Similarly Sikhs accept that animals have souls which live on and Buddhist philosophy is based upon rebirth of all life. Native American and other aboriginal cultures practice animism based on the belief that all natural objects within the universe have souls or spirits.

As with the subject of death it is to children's literature we owe a particular awareness of contemporary notions of animal afterlife. Popular books such as *Dog Heaven* (and the sequel *Cat Heaven*) by Cynthia Rylant, along with the book, *The Heaven of Animals* by Nancy Tillman offer visions of an animal paradise.[29] Some of over 600 pet cemeteries in North America even link pets to specific faith rituals.

> Science knows it doesn't know everything; otherwise, it'd stop. But just because science doesn't know everything doesn't mean you can fill in the gaps with whatever fairy tale most appeals to you.
>
> Dara Ó Briain

Sociologically, perhaps the most important aspect for humanity is the process of narrative, including parables, to constitute a form of memory which includes elements which recognize some form of afterlife. Thus all living, or ex-living, things may be considered as cultural objects through which humans may come to our own terms with death, burial and the afterlife.

There is, of course, no afterlife or heavenly paradise supported by systematic evidence or objective and explicit criteria. Human belief systems relating to death and mortality fail to fulfil Koch's postulates which relate cause and effect, thus failing the test of hard science.

Conclusions

This essay began by making the point that humans and non-human animals have more in common than not. This is not so surprising given that mammals shared a common ancestor approximately 80 million years ago. Data from the Genome Project indicate that mice and men share virtually the same genes (perhaps Steinbeck was ahead of his time). Yet the lines from Yeats' poem *Death* clearly separated humans from animals with regard to death or dying since non-humans can neither 'dread nor hope' for it. Animals are often objectified, in real life and in literature, because life scientists have taken often narrow views and social scientists for the most part remain anthropocentric.

Manners, habits and points of view, including mankind's attitudes to animals or to death have been ascribed to relative degrees of encephalization. Human attitudes to other humans are not so different as we see reflected in the Orwellian definition of tribes. Humans can and do treat other humans, tribes or races not only as friends but also as tools, demons and even vermin. All ideas have some correspondence with the facts of the time which spawned them. Of the revolutions which have been part of humankind's experience the most recent, which is scientific understanding of life's processes, is in full flood.

---

[1] Michael Faherty, *The Poetry of W.B. Yeats* (UK: Palgrave Macmillan, 2004).
[2] William M. Spellman, *A Brief History of Death* (London et al: Reaktion Books Ltd, 2014).
[3] Charles Darwin, *The Descent of Man, and Selection in Relation to Sex* (London: John Murray, 1871).
[4] Hillard S. Kaplan and Arthur J. Robson, 'The Emergence of Humans: the Coevolution of Intelligence and Longevity with Intergenerational Transfers', in *Proceedings of the National Academy of Sciences of the United States of America*, 99/15 (2002), 10221-6.
[5] Shultz, S., E. Nelson, and R.I. Dunbar, 'Hominin cognitive evolution: identifying patterns and processes in the fossil and archaeological record', in *Philosophical transactions of the Royal Society of London. Series B, Biological sciences*, 367/1599 (2012), 2130-40.
[6] Linda Kalof, *Looking at Animals in Human History* (USA: University of Chicago Press, 2007).
[7] Monica Libell, *Seeing Animals. Anthropomorphism between Fact and Function*, 2005. [cited 2017 19th February]; Available

from:www.academia.edu/8752753/Seeing Animals. Anthropomorphism between fact and function.

[8] *On the Properties of Things, John Trevisa's Translation of* Bartholomaeus Anglicus De Proprietatibus Rerum (Oxford: Oxford University Press, 1988).

[9] Benjamin Farrington, 'The Preface of Andreas Vesalius to De Fabrica Corporis Humani 1543', in *Proceedings of the Royal Society of Medicine*, 25/9 (1932), 1357-66.

[10] Paul Waldau, 'Putting the Horse before Descartes: My Life's Work on Behalf of Animals', *Anthrozoös, 26/3 (2013),* 471-3.

[11] *The Philosophical Writings of Descartes,* eds D.M. John Cottingham, Robert Stoothoff, Anthony Kenny (Cambridge: Cambridge University Press, 1991).

[12] Arnold Arluke, *et al.*, 'The Relationship of Animal Abuse to Violence and Other Forms of Antisocial Behavior', in *Journal of Interpersonal Violence,* 14/9 (1999), 963-975.

[13] World Economic Forum, *The Fourth Industrial Revolution.* 2016 [cited 2017 February]; Available from: www.weforum.org/agenda.archive/fourth-industrial-revolution.

[14] Frédéric Leroy, Peter Scholliers, and Virginie Arnilien, 'Elements of Innovation and Tradition in Meat Fermentation: Conflicts and synergies', in *International Journal of Food Microbiology*, 212 (2015), 2-8.

[15] Alan Kellehear, *A Social History of Dying* (Cambridge: Cambridge University Press, 2007).

[16] Mark Twain, *The Lowest Animal.* ed. Shelley F. Fishkin (USA: University of California Press, 2009).

[17] E.B. White, 'Death of a Pig', *The Atlantic* (1948), *Charlotte's Web* (USA: Harper & Brothers, 1952).

[18] Jean Giono, *Le grand troupeau (*France: Gallimard, 1931).

[19] Ian Colman, et al., 'CARTOONS KILL: Casualties in Animated Recreational Theater in an objective observational new study of kids' introduction to loss of life', in *British Medical Journal,* 349 (2014), g7184.

[20] Leigh Van Valen and Virginia Maiorana, 'HeLa, a new microbial species', in *Evolutionary Theory & Review*, 10 (1991), 71–74.

[21] Kristina Jennbert, 'Animal Graves: Dog, Horse and Bear', in *Current Swedish Archaeology,* 11 (2003), 139-152.

[22] Salima Ikram, 'Man's Best Friend For Eternity: Dog And Human Burials in Ancient Egypt', in *Anthropozoologica*, 48 (2013), 299-307.

[23] Stephan Mithen, *After The Ice: A Global Human History, 20,000-5000 BC.* (Cambridge MA: Harvard University Press, 2003).

[24] Finbar McCormick, 'Animal bones from prehistoric Irish burials', in *Journal of Irish Archaeology*, 3 (1986), 37-48.

[25] Laurence Flanagan, *Ancient Ireland: Life Before the Celts* (Dublin: Gill & Macmillan, 1998).

[26] Evelyn Waugh, *The Loved One* (UK: Chapman & Hall, 1948).

[27] Lynne Rudder Baker, 'Death and the Afterlife', in *The Oxford Handbook of Philosophy of Religion,* ed. W.J. Wainwright (UK: Oxford University Press, 2007).

[28] Yuval Noah Harari, *Homo Deus: A Brief History of Tomorrow* (London, Harper, 2015)*; Sapiens: A Brief History of Humankind* (London: Harvill Secker, 2015).

[29] Cynthia Ryland, *Dog Heaven* (New York: Blue Sky Press, 1995), *Cat Heaven* (New York: Blue Sky Press, 1997). Nancy Tillman, *The Heaven of Animals* (New York: Feiwel & Friends, 2014).

7 | Ignoring Death – War, Maps and Advertising

Joseph Brady

'War is hell' said General William Tecumseh Sherman during the American Civil War, and that neat summation is one that would command general agreement. That being the case, it might be somewhat surprising that war holds such a fascination. War movies are immensely popular, novels equally so and many people will discuss in great detail the intricacies of military campaigns and famous battles. And this is not just among the members of military history societies; there is a general level of interest and knowledge in the population that is more than casual.

Despite the terrible carnage of war and the many personal tragedies that result, war is often remembered fondly. Tom Lehrer, who might be said to offer a somewhat cynical view of the world, once introduced his song, 'So long Mom, I'm off to drop the bomb'[1] by noting that 'World War II produced many hit songs, though it was not primarily a musical. We sing the songs because we like to remember how much we enjoyed the war'.

This seeming paradox is beloved of professionals of all varieties who attempt to explain it in a number of ways. The paper that people turn to for an early statement of the issue is William James' *The Moral Equivalent of War*, delivered as a lecture in 1906 and published in 1910.[2] In essence, his argument is not too far distant from the sentiments expressed by Tom Lehrer. War is seen to bring out the best in people. The civic processes of the state are focused on a single purpose and people feel engaged with that purpose. As James put it: 'to show war's irrationality and horror has no effect upon him. The horrors make the fascination. War is the strong life; it is life *in extremis*. War taxes are the only ones men never hesitate to pay, as the budgets of all nations show'. This, however, does not explain the reasons for going to war. Evolutionary biologists suggest that it lies in the realm of the selfish gene. They point out that there are few societies which have never gone to war and that it is about dominance, pride and the control of others.[3]

The key therefore is that war is ennobled. In war is seen the epitome of heroic virtues and the symbols of war are often used to express the nation. A 'state funeral', for example, often involves the bearing of the body on a gun carriage. Monarchs adopt military uniforms when they undertake civic duties. Countries are spoken of as the 'fatherland' or the 'motherland' and the defence of that from which the nation springs is surely the highest civic duty.

Nor is this merely a preoccupation of a ruling class who might have a particular interest in the territorial integrity of a country. It permeates deep into society through the education system or, at least it did until recently. The stories of the Horatii on the bridge or the 300 at Thermopylae were part of the staple instruction of children in the Western world. Indeed, in a local context, the patriotic ballad, *A Nation Once Again*, written by Thomas Davis in the 1840s,[4] captures these references as the singer recalls that:

> when boyhood's fire was in my blood, I read of ancient freemen
> for Greece and Rome who bravely stood, three hundred men
> and three men.

However, the most powerful of these exhortations came from Horace and his Ode (III.2.13) in which he exhorts Rome to develop its power so that nobody would dare to resist them. The phrase which everyone learned was 'Dulce et decorum est pro patria mori' and it was explained that it was a sweet and noble thing to die for one's country. Even in the modern era, this view was rarely challenged and it was rather unlikely that the poem of the same title by Wilfred Owen[5] in which he describes the impact of a gas attack during World War I would be offered as a counterweight.

> If in some smothering dreams, you too could pace
> Behind the wagon that we flung him in,
> And watch the white eyes writhing in his face,
> His hanging face, like a devil's sick of sin,
> If you could hear, at every jolt, the blood
> Come gargling from the froth-corrupted lungs
> Bitter as the cud
> Of vile, incurable sores on innocent tongues, –
> My friend, you would not tell with such high zest
> To children ardent for some desperate glory,
> The old Lie: Dulce et decorum est
> Pro patria mori.

This description of the reality of death is that from which people distance themselves. This is the reality of war which society chooses not to engage with or at least to forget as quickly as possible. The comments by British Prime Minister, Margaret Thatcher at the Falklands victory parade in 1982 were very much in this mould. She said:

> In those anxious months the spectacle of bold young Britons, fighting for great principles and a just cause, lifted the nation. Throughout our land our people were inspired. Doubt and

hesitation were replaced by confidence and pride that our generation could write a glorious chapter in the history of liberty.⁶

This forgetfulness permits the engagement with the heroic but sometimes this has to be managed. Lest people focus on the horror and not on the victory, it was initially decided not to allow the wounded and disabled to parade in the Falklands victory parade on 12 October 1982. As the *Guardian Weekly* reported it: 'there were a token number of disabled servicemen at the Falklands victory parade in London on Tuesday. Some officials didn't want there to be any at all'.⁷ Earlier in July, the Church of England came in for stinging criticism because it would not allow the word 'victory' to be used in the service and the Archbishop of Canterbury had struck a discordant note when he said that 'war is a sign of human failure and everything we say and do in this service must be in this context'.⁸

Thus far it might be argued that war is primarily the business of men and it is men who generally prosecute wars. The argument might be advanced therefore that this is a gendered view of society and that matters might be different in a society where men and women are truly equal. While it is true that women (generally) do not go to war, that may be no more than an absence of opportunity. There is some evidence to suggest that women are not immune to the same stirrings of nobility.

Plutarch, writing about Sparta, noted the sayings of the Spartan women. They are replete with mothers requiring the ultimate sacrifice of their sons and being angered when this is not freely given. The best known is what a mother said to her son on the occasion of presenting him with his shield: 'Either with this or upon this'.⁹

Now it might be argued that Sparta was different. Its society was structured as a big military camp and, in the absence of a good primary record, the sayings of the Spartan women may be taken at less than face value. What is not in question though comes from more recent history. Women played a very active role in persuading men to do the right thing during WWI. In the absence of conscription it was necessary to appeal to the innate honour and valour of the menfolk. They joined in large numbers without prompting but some were less convinced. 'Your King and Country want you' was a popular song from 1914 and was sung with enthusiasm by Helen Clark.¹⁰ The Order of the White Feather sent many to the trenches in WWI when their innate common sense would have told them that this was not a particularly good idea. Granted the organization was begun by a man in 1914, Admiral Charles Fitzgerald, but it was promoted enthusiastically by women. In fact, so effective were they at distributing white feathers that, to avoid harassment, civil servants and

Fig. 7.1) Examples of 'War Service badge' designed to show that the bearer was involved in essential duties.

others engaged in work of national importance had to be given badges (Fig. 7.1) proclaiming that they were working for King and country.[11]

It is possible to summarize by suggesting that, despite the horrors of war of which everyone is aware, it has held a fascination for us down through the centuries. It stirs something in society and even if people are not directly involved in a war, they can appreciate, understand, and take an interest in other people's wars. But it is much easier to do so if the unpleasant aspects of war, the horror of death and the disfigurement of the wounded is ignored as much as possible while the public is confronted at most with individual, 'heroic' deaths.

Satisfying the Interest

Books about war have always done well with the general public. Armchair generals have always been eager to discuss the finer detail of military campaigns. Caesar's *Gallic Wars* would have been a bestseller in their day had printing been around. The advent of mass-market printing in the nineteenth century allowed the general population to follow up-to-the-minute reports about the wars of the time. Both *The Graphic* and the *Illustrated London News* provided weekly reports for their readers and for the first time illustrations were available, adding to the ideas of derring do and heroism. Illustrations were a very important part of the news. Readers avidly bought copies of the *Illustrated London News* for its etchings of Balaclava and the example here shows that these images had no issue with emphasizing the mayhem and carnage (Fig. 7.2).[12] It was during the Zulu war of 1879 that the power of weekly reports with drawings

Ignoring Death: War, Maps and Advertising

Fig. 7.2) The charge of the light cavalry at Balaclava.

was seen as teams of war artists were sent to the region so that the weekly editions were properly illustrated.[13] Engravings of great generals or depictions of battles might of interest but this is a circumstance where the map comes into its own. Wars, by their nature, are intensely geographical. They are generally about the contesting of space and the drawing of lines on maps. They take place over the landscape and the characteristics of that landscape play an essential role in strategy and tactics. If the reader is to follow a war, he *must* have a map. The ILN and other publishers were quick to meet this need. Maps accompanied the graphics and supplements were produced showing the shifting lines. Many of these were big enough to be displayed on walls and there seems to have been an expectation that somewhere in the home would be the map room.

At the same time, the map was utterly safe and removed the user from any need to contemplate the reality of suffering and death. People tend not to feature on maps; maps are patterns of shapes and lines, expressed in a variety of colours. There is no need to contemplate the horror of war, rather it can be seen as a board game. Indeed, some of the maps described below were expressly designed to be used in this way with all of the family engaged in sticking flags on maps or drawing lines of advance and retreat. As the producer of the Dated Events War Map (discussed later) put it, you could 'Book your seat in the theatre of war'.

Fig. 7.3) Cover of the Liberty Map of the Western Front.

The use of maps became more sophisticated as time went on but, to begin with, they tended to have an immediate association with the entity that was producing them. Thus, it was not unexpected that the Fédération des Automobile Clubs Régionaux de France would produce a series of maps of World War I showing the various fronts — and not just in France. There was, for example, a map of northern France, carte-guide Campbell No. 2, at a scale of 1:320,000 which showed the front as of March 1917 and October 1917. These days, the *Literary Digest* is remembered more for its disastrous results prediction for the 1936 US Presidential election.[14] However, before that it was an important and influential US magazine noted for its opinion articles and analysis of contemporary events. It too felt that its readers would enjoy maps of the conflict, even though the United States was not then a belligerent. Most impressive was its 'Liberty Map of the Western Front' (Fig. 7.3) which came with a full index whose cover suggests the excitement of war. This map was over 4 feet by 3 feet (1.2 x 0.9m) in size on waxed paper with a linen backing. It was clearly intended for display because it was not manageable otherwise.

The First World War for all its brutality and death did not permit the map to be exploited to its full commercial extent. The Western front line

Fig. 7.4) Covers of maps in a *Daily Express* set.

did not change enough over the months to justify the making of regular editions but it did prove the concept that there was a market for information on the war.[15] By the time of the Second World War, marketing was far better developed as a business concept and the commercialization potential of maps had been fully realized. It was realized that people were hungry for information and that they were prepared to buy products that provided it. Thus, what was counter intuitive, namely that a product be associated with death, destruction, sorrow and slaughter became an important marketing tool. Normally products go to great lengths to ensure that the image that they present is one of probity, health and the promotion of a 'good time'. War seems an unlikely activity as an advertising opportunity. Yet, for the reasons described above, war became increasingly seen as an opportunity to advertise and the favoured medium for this in the period to the end of the Second World War was the map.

Great Britain and the United States

There is a contrast to be made between Great Britain and the United States. The production of these war maps was concentrated in the USA. Maps were produced in Britain during the period of the war but they were relatively few in number and the overt commercialization was absent.

They were mainly produced by the newspapers though there was a detailed series of maps produced for the specialist on a weekly basis.[16] The *Daily Express* produced a map of the Western front (Fig. 7.4) and one of the Mediterranean for which an updated 'second front' edition was produced. There was also a map of Scandinavia. The *Daily Telegraph* had a set of nine maps while the *Daily Mail*, together with a range of maps, produced a *War Atlas* of 32 pages of 'coloured maps covering every area of land, sea and air operations' and the *News Chronicle* was not to be outdone. The most obvious reason for the difference was that paper was a scarce commodity but, given what has been argued above, it could also be the case that the distance from the theatre of war in the USA allowed people to take that more detached view of war which permitted its commercialization. The United States was under no threat of invasion and was beyond the range of any aircraft of the time (as many maps helpfully showed). There was the possibility of U-boat attack on coastal locations but this was more a danger to shipping than to settlement. The Sunoco company, while making the point in their *War Planes and Air Lanes* map that their high octane fuel was now reserved entirely for the military, provided a graphic showing German war planes, their associated statistics, and helpful silhouettes which 'will allow you to quickly

Fig. 7.5) Detail from the cover of the Hammond War Map Kit.

recognize any plane', knowing full well that most people would never see such planes.

The first group to engage actively with map production were the commercial map companies. These already had base maps to hand and it was an easy task to turn these into special editions for the war. All of the major companies were involved, such as Geographica, Rand McNally, Hammond, Hagstrom, and each produced a variety of maps at different scale as well as war atlases, an activity which increased as the war neared its conclusion. Hagstrom's maps, for example, invited the owner to 'Follow the war'. Rand McNally produced a war atlas in 1944 which they offered to update free-of-charge once the post-war shape of the world was fixed.

All companies produced maps with a global focus, a focus on Europe and a focus on the Far-East, and it is clear that they had a variety of lines on the go at the same time. Geographica had in 1944 a total of 36 'timely' maps. Perhaps half of these were pre-war maps which simply were given a new spin by being called 'War maps of ...' but the remainder were maps that had been specifically produced to provide news on the war such as the 'strategical' map of the world.

Not to be outdone, the Hammond company had a similar range but it went a little further in that it produced a boxed *War Map Kit* (Fig. 7.5). This was a range of resources that would provide complete coverage of the war in a nice cardboard box. The kit contained a world-wide war atlas, two world maps showing different aspects of the war, a series of battle maps including maps of Europe and the Far East. These maps had a nice touch in that in the margins were little flags that could be cut out and by the insertion of a pin could be turned into campaign markers. In addition, there was a 'hand vest pocket atlas' — more on this below — and various sheets on which to record important events. It was quite a comprehensive undertaking and it turned the war into something akin to a sports league with tables of scores.

These maps shared the characteristic that they were for sale. However, the main interest of this paper is in the maps which were designed to be handed out free of charge to customers. Having them for sale would have undermined their value as commercial and advertising media. The range of companies who did this kind of thing was enormous.

The opportunites were obvious for companies with a direct involvement in or connection to the war. Oil companies were quick to see the advantage as were others which produced war materials such as engineering companies, ship builders and even food suppliers. Some companies produced maps themselves, those from Esso were the most sophisticated, but most availed of a service offered by publishing companies such as Rand

Fig. 7.6) The customizing for the *Allied Liberty Map of the World at War*.

McNally and Hammond whereby they took a map that was generally available and they customized it to be identified with a particular industry. Sometimes the customizing was crude.

Take for example, the *Allied Liberty Map of the World at War* produced by the P.D. Hall company (Fig. 7.6). It was a one-sided map, slightly smaller than A2 in size and it showed the world on a Mercator grid. The image here shows it customized by the sticking of a paper label on the bottom of the map, in this case for a book store. Most times, though, customization was a sophisticated operation whereby you, as the company, were able to offer a well-designed map of the world.

There are no data on the number of these maps produced but it must have run into millions. If survival is anything to go by, the Esso maps were the most numerous. These were produced between 1942 and 1944, at about A2 size. A first map dealing with Transportation was followed by a map of Europe and then by a map of the Pacific (Fig. 7.7). The map of Europe was updated to reflect the invasion in 1944. They were also the most impressive in terms of content and they aimed to educate each user. Each map was accompanied by text boxes that explained such things as reading distances on a projection, how projections were used and how the geography of global warfare was going to work out. The maps themselves departed from the standard Mercator projection which gave a distorted impression of the relative areas of countries while being true in directional terms. Instead, they made use of a projection made by O.M. Miller of the American Geographical Society of New York. This was absolutely up to date having been presented by Miller only in 1942.[17] The projection reduces the distortions of the Mercator map for higher latitudes and allows the poles to be shown but introduces such other errors as to make it useful only for display purposes. Esso had clearly gone to significant trouble to ensure that their maps displayed to best advantage. They also introduced new concepts — they spoke of the 'world island' and 'Fortress Europe'; terms which have passed into common speech.

Ignoring Death: War, Maps and Advertising

Fig. 7.7) Two Esso maps, one an 'invasion edition'.

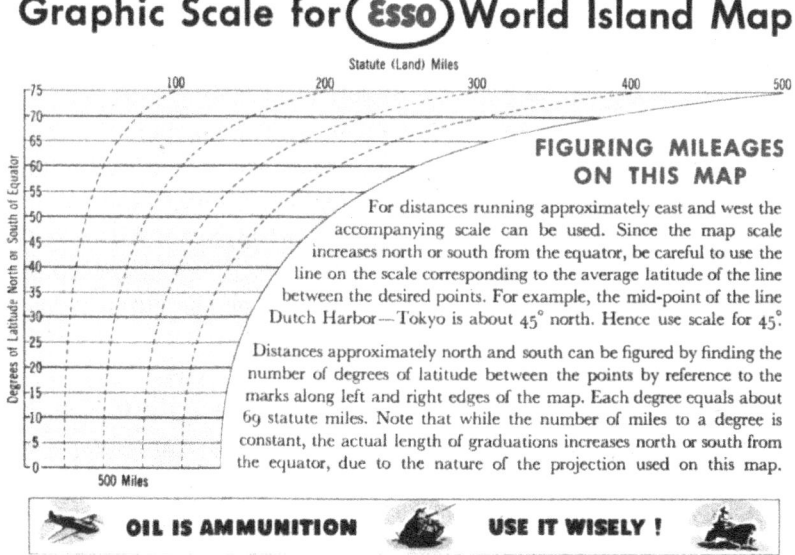

Fig. 7.8) Information panel from the Esso 'World Island' map.

Their *War Map II*, which focused on Europe, offered an essay entitled the 'geography of global warfare' in which it was explained that a new perspective was needed to understand wars which had global reach. This was provided in the ideas of H.J. Mackinder who

> published certain novel theories as to the influence of geography on history and more particularly on military history. Instead of considering the world in the conventional manner as divided into continents, he looked at it realistically as consisting of one principal land mass surrounded by water and scattered islands. This main body includes what we are accustomed to call Europe, Asia and Africa, and to it he gave the name World Island. (See 'Democratic Ideals and Reality' by Sir Halford J. Mackinder, republished, 1942, by Henry Holt and Company, New York, $2.50.) He asserted that any country which became master of Eastern Europe could control this World Island and eventually the entire world.

It will be noted that this was a properly referenced essay and there was no attempt to patronize the reader. This and others were solid geographical essays, obviously well considered and brought geography to the fore in the understanding of these events (Fig. 7.8). The maps themselves were well-drawn with topography shown in hachuring. Towns and cities were located, major oil fields and distances between important locations were shown. These essays and information panels were combined with marketing information about Esso and its role in the war. This indicated that the company produced more than oil and petrol. They produced a range of chemicals and products from delousing powder to tarpaulins for tents.

Other maps focused more on tactical matters. The *International Radio News Map*, produced for the Don Lee Broadcasting system by Rand McNally (Fig. 7.9), showed areas of occupied territory, the maximum range of various aircraft (the USA was well out of range of anything flying) and other important data for the armchair general. The British convoy routes were shown, the maximum range of US patrols as well as distances and locations of strategic resources.

Other oil companies such as Richfield Oil, Pure Oil, Philips 66 or Sinclair Gasoline produced maps. Airlines saw value in the idea, as did Aloco aluminium and companies making radios. The Aloco map was particularly interesting in that it provided details of the markings of aircraft including those for Éire.[18] A more unusual one was that for Linton's Bristols which it was suggested 'attracts and holds attention' and 'stands up and stands out'! The connection with radio was another obvious link, either by itself or in combination with some other war

Ignoring Death: War, Maps and Advertising

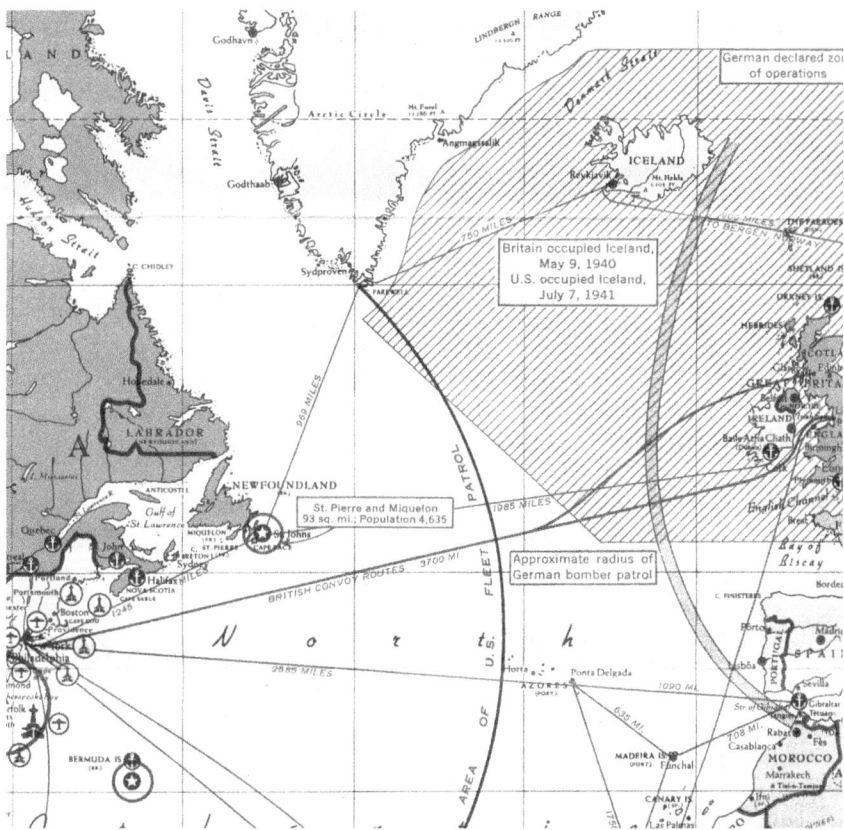

Fig. 7.9) Detail from the International Radio News map, showing ranges.

industry. Some oil companies, Pure Oil for example, linked their maps with particular commentators on the radio. Thus the driver was invited to use their Pure Oil map while listening to H.V Kaltenborn. He was a respected commentator on world affairs for over 30 years beginning with CBS in 1928. The linkage was assured by entitling the map 'Kaltenborn's New War Map produced by the Pure Oil company of Chicago'. The Esso Transportation map listed a set of radio stations where regular broadcasts could be heard. Not to be outdone, the Sunoco oil company associated their map with the broadcaster Lowell Thomas. Thomas was also a veteran broadcaster, credited with having brought Lawrence of Arabia to public notice and was at the time exploiting the possibilities of television as well as continuing as a respected radio man.

Some maps were designed for those with a serious interest. The Serial Map Service offered a monthly bulletin on the progress of the war which combined well-argued papers by experts with high quality maps of the region in debate. The papers discussed military tactics, geopolitics and the issues associated with map production, such as questions of the most suitable map projections. This was available on an annual subscription of 32s. 6d., for which a binder was supplied. This was a UK production and its social value was clearly recognized by the authorities in that they advertised that they had a licence to post the bulletin overseas.

For others, following the war was meant to be a fun activity. The Rand McNally *Master War Map of the World* was your home strategist pin-up map. This was designed to involve all the family and there was nothing sombre about the image of the mother, father and the children plotting the progress of the war together and doubtless discussing the value and virtue of the various decisions taken.

Customization

The production of these maps was a big and expensive undertaking and not easily done by companies without the resources of oil companies. It was clear that people were very interested in the war and marketing executives were quick to see that a service could be offered to other companies that would allow them to capitalize on the patriotic fervour and associate the company's product or service with a noble activity but at much lower cost. The selling point was that when the war ended, the company's service would get a bit of the reflected glory that comes to the victors and so prosper.

The link between maps and radio stations has already been made above. Radio stations in the United States were in competition and there were many local private stations. Advertising followed listeners and how better to get the listeners than to produce a local version of a map. Take the example of the *'Invasion Issue' Global War Map*. The WHO radio station on 1040 kilocycles of Des Moines Iowa was one of many companies who chose this map to advertise. They told their listeners about their own broadcasts and when they could catch national relays. 'For authentic war news, keep turned to WHO — 1040 kilocycles, your only Iowa radio station with worldwide NBC coverage', the map advised.[19]

But radio was not the only linkage possible. The maps were produced to make a linkage between the war and all sorts of products (Fig. 7.10). Thus, the same map was used to advertise Champagne Velvet Pilsner, the beer with the 'million dollar flavor' produced in Terre Haute, Indiana. The company did not even attempt to make a linkage between drinking beer and the war effort. There were many such maps and an even wider range of products that used them.[20] After all, the consumer could not be expected to rely on one map only. There was also the Rand McNally map that showed military and naval power. One element was a detailed tactical

Ignoring Death: War, Maps and Advertising

Fig. 7.10) Two versions of the Rand McNally map.

Fig. 7.11) Staley's and the Military and Naval Map of World War II.

map, showing the current geopolitical situation, the distance from various locations to the coast of the United States and the all-important indication of the maximum range of German bombers. There was a general version and a customized version. This example is for Staley's, and on this occasion they tried to make a connection between their products and the war by declaring that they were 'geared for the emergency'. Besides offering a handy guide to the different world time zones, it is hard to see how they might have explicitly been geared to the emergency since it appeared that they produced corn starch and laundry starch. If the company had their tongues firmly in their cheeks, there might have been a connection between the war and Staley's waffle syrup since no war could be without waffle (Fig. 7.11). However, that seems unlikely and the customer was instead invited to enjoy the extra sweetness in waffles made with this syrup since it was high in dextrose and maltose, 'those energy sugars needed so much in emergencies'.

The Sears company also pursued the link with radio but this time they wanted to sell them. Their map, quite a good one with lots of detail on the relative strengths of the various armies which also included a schematic of the Maginot line, pushed the purchase of a 'Silvertone' radio that would allow you to keep up to date.

As noted above, most maps were high quality and much thought and effort went into the design. In some cases the standard slipped. The Palmolive (made with olive oil!) company made the connection between soap and warfare by issuing a set of three maps in 1940. There was one for the Balkan Peninsula, one for the Western Front and one for the British Isles. The positioning of towns was a little odd and they seemed to believe that Dún Laoghaire was still Kingstown and that Cobh and Queenstown were separate places. Other offerings were no more than pre-war copies where the European theatre, for example, was no more than a map of Europe with an action-packed cover on the front.

Map Sizes

To assist in the marketing process, maps came in all sizes and shapes. The wall map was very popular with a size of A1 to A3 being common. These were for display at home, especially the ones which offered the opportunity to pin flags to the various positions. They were also supplied at desktop size, where they could be referred to while reading the newspaper or listening to the radio. They also came in tiny sizes, which is both wonderful and baffling. The one that appeals most is the pocket atlas, barely larger than a credit card in size but containing 16 full colour maps of the world. This came as part of the Hammond map set described above, but it was also available as a standalone mini-atlas. The example here was customized for Enro shirts, sportswear and pyjamas. They invited the user to view their 'victory line' for Fall 1942 (Fig. 7.12). Doubtless this size of atlas was useful for any urgent or emergency discussion.

War, Advertising and Sales

The paper has yet to show that there was a conscious and explicit link being made between the war, maps, advertising, the desire to capitalize on patriotic fervour and future sales. Certainly that link is implicitly present in the maps as an examination of the Esso maps will make clear. They make the point that oil and the products of oil are crucial to the winning of the war and that is a goal that everyone would support. From

Fig. 7.12) The Erno mini-atlas.

there it is but a simple syllogism. The Esso company is an oil company. So one should support the Esso Company. The maps were very well designed and attractive and, as discussed above, were highly educative but for all of their information they conveyed no sense of the horrors of war. In their *Invasion Edition* map featuring 'The World Island' and 'Fortress Europe' there is a graphic of US aircraft on a bombing raid over a harbour with oil installations on fire and a much smaller one of ships at sea. One information panel noted that 'the face of world is changing. Countries have come – and gone. Boundaries have changed ...' but there was no sense that there might be a human cost in the disappearance of boundaries or indeed countries. There was naturally no reference to death, destruction, starvation or refugees. The nearest that Esso came to suggesting that their wartime activities might come with a human cost was in their *Transportation* map. Here there is a graphic (Fig. 7.13) showing a city in flames under the heading 'Bombs for Berlin, Terror for Toyko'. The balance was quickly restored, though, for while Esso was proud to have developed toluol, crucial in explosives, it was also pointed out that Esso developed plastics; a new insecticide that meant that the 'only safe place for such vermin [was] behind enemy lines'; was defeating rust; had produced new grades of wax for skis; eliminated mildew from tarpaulins and found its products used in 'healing lotions'. Thus Esso was

Fig. 7.13) Detail from the Esso Transportation map.

intimately bound up in the business of war and was proud of it. The making of better bombs was to be understood in the context of a diverse contribution to the war effort with products which were innocent, benign and needed.

The other oil companies did much the same. The sense of buying goodwill becomes more explicit in this Fred Harvey's map. This was a family owned company, which grew from the nineteenth century endeavours of its founder and is credited as being the first 'chain' of restaurants in the American south west. The company was known for innovation in marketing and was not going to pass up the opportunity offered by these maps. There were three maps in a folder; a map of the world at war, a map of the United States and one that that concentrated on battle insignia. This map makes the point that the company was giving special service to those in the armed forces.

> To our guests – the servicemen: We hope this pocket folder will be of interest to you. Our managers and employees are proud to serve you and have been requested, in so far as conditions permit, to give you second helpings if you want them. When the war is won; when food rationing, so essential now, is no longer necessary; when hundreds of Harvey-trained men and women, now in the Armed Forces, are with us again ... then we hope that you will come back and dine more leisurely and enjoy the kind of hospitality we like to offer our friends.

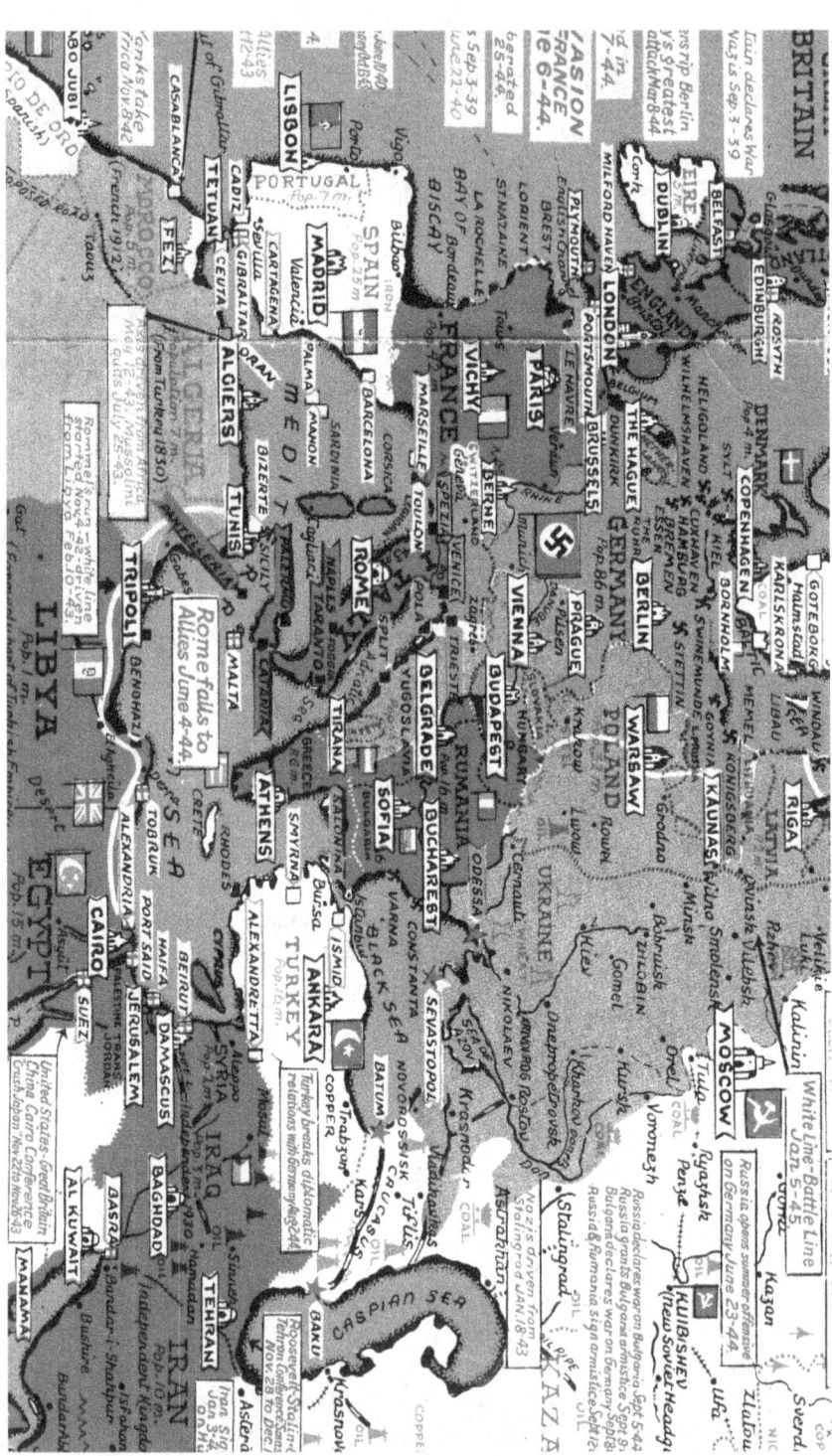

Fig. 7.14) Detail from Dated War Map.

The link between war, maps, advertising and business was made explicit, however, in a set of maps produced throughout the war by, among others, the Gettier Montanye company of Baltimore in Maryland. This is an advertising company who have been in business since 1922 and in their present-day incarnation make promotional products including clothing, hats, food, candy and gadgets which can be personalized as required. After 1943, their product was what they called a 'dated events' war map. In essence this was a map of the world, about 1m long by 0.5 m high, on a Mercator grid. On it were shown the major events of the war and the date on which they happened (Fig. 7.14).[21] The scope for updates was enormous and they took every opportunity that arose to produce one.

```
The Greatest War Map Ever
Designed - Provides You a Top Flight
Goodwill Salesman for Your Business

This is your opportunity to assure customer goodwill and loyalty for your
business during the war and after the war. Put your name and your business
on "Dated Events" - the most sensational map of the war.

You simply must see this famous war map to really appreciate it. Unfold the
enclosed sample and judge for yourself. Note the exclusive and copyrighted
"Dated Events" feature, found in no other map. Never before have you seen a
map just like it.

Colorful, informative, authentic, "Dated Events" is really more than a map.
It is a highly condensed and concise history of the war. Everything that
happened on the battlefields of Europe and Asia is recorded right on this
map - with names, dates and places. Everything from Munich to D-Day, in-
cluding the Liberation of France, the surprise attack by Germany, the great
Russian advances, America's mighty offensives in Asia and the Pacific.

This isn't all by a long shot! This famous war map also gives you bombing
distances between world capitols, naval and air bases, world raw material
sources, supply routes, an enlarged map of Nazi Germany. A new edition is
just going to press. That's the map you will get.

You will be proud to distribute this new "Dated Events" war map with your
business imprint, among your many good customers and friends - perhaps em-
ployees. It will bring you much goodwill and prestige both now and after
the war. At these low direct prices, you can afford to be generous in its
distribution. Prices are on the enclosed order form.

However, with present paper restrictions in force, all we can say is be very
prompt with your order. We will try to fill them on a first come, first
served basis, while present supplies last.

Make sure - mail your order today.

                                        Sincerely yours,

                                        C. N. Montanye
                                        C. N. Montanye, Pres.
15M 1-15-45                             GETTIER-MONTANYE, INC.
```

Fig. 7.15) Gettier Montayne letter to potential customers.

Fig. 7.16) Some examples of Dated War Maps.

The idea was that individual businesses would purchase quantities of these maps, overprinted with their logo or business name. They could then be sent out to the individual customers of these companies. In the blurb that was sent out to potential purchasers in January 1945, companies were advised that (Fig. 7.15):

> This is your opportunity to assure customer goodwill and loyalty for your business during the war and after the war. Put your name and your business on 'Dated Events' – the most sensational map of the war.

> You will be proud to distribute this new 'Dated Events' war map with your business imprint, among your many good customers

and friends – perhaps employees. It will bring you much goodwill and prestige both now and after the war. At these low direct prices, you can afford to be generous in its distribution.

The maps were on offer in a special envelope for 10.5 cents each, based on a print-run of 10,000 or more with the price rising to 15.5 cents each if fewer than 150 were printed. All was designed to make it easy for the company to ship to their customers. All that was needed was a label and a stamp.

Later in 1944, they produced the 21st edition, designed to show the 'Invasion Map of Fortress Europe' and they noted that 'the series of maps has accurately and dramatically portrayed the geographical and historical happenings of this great war. It has proven to be an outstanding advertising piece for the many thousands of firms who have used it'.

There are no data available on how many copies of the various editions of the map were printed, but the fact that a print-run of 10,000 or more was provided for on the order form is indicative of the scale of the activity. What is clear from the survivals is that the offer was taken up by myriad companies (Fig. 7.16). There are examples from a construction company, a hospital linen company, an insurance company, a battery company, a sporting goods company, a jewellery company and United Air Lines. The reach of the company was national and there are examples from Ohio, Illinois, Pennsylvania, North Carolina, Missouri, Texas and California. The Gettier company was not the only company offering this map or this service. In fact, the production operation was international in that the Gettier company did not produce the maps themselves. They were produced by the CC Peterson Company of Toronto in Canada, itself an advertising company, who produced a number of versions of the dated war map for different businesses, though the most successful seems to have been the version that they produced for Gettier Montanye.

A Successful Formula?

With the end of the Second World War, so ended this particular episode where cartography was centre-stage in bringing news of a global war into households far from the action and, indeed the daily horrors. Maps had been used in a multi-faceted way capitalizing (in all senses of the word) on our fascination with war, our insatiable thirst for knowledge, our belief that, despite its horrors, it is a noble activity. The user was invited to ignore the bloody business of war and the reality that it involved death on an industrial scale and instead to think of war as an educational activity and perhaps even an entertainment. It was never expressed in

Fig. 7.17) The *Daily Express* Second Front Series. Note the provision of gummed symbols to make the map interactive.

such a crass manner and instead it was suggested that it was the fact that war was something that had to be done, that had to be endured for the greater good that provided the licence to become involved as an armchair general. People could be solemn while exploring the detail! It was, of course, a sanitized involvement and this was all the more so in the United States where the bulk of the maps were produced. But the maps were produced in the UK as well and here the realities of war were much closer to home. After all, the Daily Express Second Front War Maps (Fig. 7.17) provided the owner with a sheet of gummed arrows which could indicate landing points and the relative positions of armies on a day to day basis as well as 'bombs' which could indicate bombed areas.

That it was seen as an important sales and marketing opportunity is clear from the extent to which companies of all sorts and scales became involved in the business of map making. This ranged from multinational oil companies to small bakeries in Indiana and it involved all of the major geographical publishing houses. It was a most unusual and fascinating combination of geography, cartography, marketing, advertising and death!

The process was not repeated in the subsequent wars. There are some examples from the Korean War but nothing on the scale of what was produced for the Second World War. This did not represent a change in attitudes to war. Television now provided an immediacy which could not be matched by the two-dimensional world of the map. Advertising on television, especially in association with news and current affairs programmes provided the same kind of linkage but without the effort or cost of map making. There are no examples of such maps associated with the Vietnam War but that war was ambiguous in terms of motive and outcome; not the best place for an advertiser.

---

[1] *So Long, Mom (A Song for WW III)* is found on *That Was the Year That Was* (1965), a live album recorded at the hungry i in San Francisco. The introduction was part of a live performance in Olso in 1967 and was recorded by The Norwegian Broadcasting Corporation. See 'The Tom Lehrer Wisdom Channel' on Youtube.
[2] William James 'The moral equivalent of war', *McClure's Magazine* (August, 1910), 463-68.
[3] L. LeShan, *The Psychology of War: Comprehending its Mystique and its Madness* (USA: Helios Press, 2002) offers a non-technical discussion of the issue.
[4] Thomas Davis, the founder of the Young Ireland movement wrote *A Nation Once Again* in the early 1840s. It was published in *the Nation* on 13 July 1844.
[5] Wilfred Owen was an officer in the Manchester regiment during the First World War. He is regarded as one of the finest war poets of the period. He was killed on 4 November 1918. See, for example, D. Roberts, *Out in the Dark: Poetry of the First World War in Context* (UK: Saxon Books, 1998).
[6] *The Irish Times*, 13 October 1982, 5.
[7] *The Guardian*, 17 October, 1982, 10.
[8] *The Irish Times*, 27 July 1982, 5.
[9] See, for example, Volume III of the Loeb Classical Library edition, 1931.
[10] *Your King and Country want you* was a popular song written by Paul Rubens and published in 1914. It was most associated with Helen Clark, Bessie Jones and Edna Thornton and became an important recruiting song. A recording is available on Youtube at youtu.be/EwMblYM29Kc
[11] The use and availability of 'on war service' badges changed during the course of the war. Individual firms and industries issued their own badges at first but later these were deemed illegal and an official badge introduced.
[12] *The Illustrated London News*, 23 December 1854, 676-7.
[13] R. Lock, and P. Quantrill, *The 1879 Zulu war through the Eyes of the Illustrated London News* (South Africa: 30 Degrees South Publishers, 2008).
[14] With a sample of 2.5 million it still managed to get it wrong in a two horse race and predicted a win for Landon. It became a classic example in market research of how not to undertake research because the sample was inherently biased toward the better-off, being based on its subscribers.
[15] Those produced included *The Complete War Map of Western Europe* by Doubleday, W. and A.K. Johnston's *European War Map*, Bacon's *War Map of Europe*, the *News of the World War Map of the Western Front* and Rand McNally's *War Map of the Battleground of Liberty*.
[16] See the later discussion of the Serial Map Service.
[17] All maps are a compromise between aspects such as correct areal depiction, shape distortion or direction finding and the problem is particularly acute with global maps. The classic Mercator projection shows shape correctly and bearings are accurate but area becomes hugely distorted away from the standard parallel, usually the equator, to the point that it is not possible to show the polar regions. In the Miller projection, shape is minimally distorted between the 45th parallels but this distortion increases toward the poles. Land masses are stretched – more east–west than they are north–south. Bearings and distance are not correct except at the equator.

[18] This was really specialist 'anorak' information because there was next to no chance that any such plane would ever be seen. The fleet during World War II was small and, in any case, was not involved in any belligerent activity.

[19] Other stations included WIBW, the voice of Kansas, WJR from Michigan, BLZ from Denver, WHO from Des Moines. KXL broadcasters of Portland did not wait to get their 'invasion' issue customized and simply stamped a generic map.

[20] Insurance was another popular product.

[21] This particular example is from the twenty-third edition, printed in 1944. It is full colour and the black and white image here does not do it justice.

8 | Brecht and Weill's *Berliner Requiem* as a Necropolitical Statement

Wolfgang Marx

In 1928, ten years after the end of the First World War, Kurt Weill received a commission for a new composition from the Reichs-Rundfunk-Gesellschaft (Reich Broadcasting Corporation), a national organization representing regional broadcasting stations. It was initially – as the *Berliner Morgenpost* announced – to be called 'Memorial tablets, epitaphs and Death songs' and would 'treat, among other things, the death of the French aviators Nungesser and Coli as well as the lives of famous athletes.'[1] However, in the end Weill chose to write a piece that would commemorate both the end of the war as well as the subsequent failed Spartacist revolt.[2] Despite its title, the *Berliner Requiem* does not use the text of the Latin mass for the dead but is instead based on poems by Bertolt Brecht, at that time a close collaborator of the composer. Weill had met Brecht in March 1927, and their fruitful collaboration had quickly resulted in the 'Songspiel' *Mahagonny* in July 1927 (which was expanded to the full-scale opera *Aufstieg und Fall der Stadt Mahagonny / Rise and Fall of the City of Mahagonny* between 1927-9), followed in 1928 by the *Dreigroschenoper / Threepenny Opera*. Weill composed the music of the *Berliner Requiem* in November and December 1928, yet the radio authorities were uncomfortable with the work and delayed its airing which was originally scheduled for 22 February 1929. Eventually it was premiered in Frankfurt/Main on 22 May 1929 with Hans Grahl, Johannes Willy and Jean Stern as soloists, accompanied by the Orchestra of the Frankfurt Radio under the baton of Ludwig Rottenberg. Dedicated to the Frankfurt Broadcasting Station, it was only broadcast in South-West Germany, and this should remain the work's only performance during Weill and Brecht's lifetimes – Berlin would not get to hear 'its' requiem for a long time.

On 17 May 1929 – five days prior to the performance – Weill published an explanatory three-page 'Note Concerning *Das Berliner Requiem*' in which he outlined the piece's purpose.[3] In this note he called the work a cantata for the concert hall 'which can also be performed just as well in the theatre through the gestic fixing of content and through the attempted vividness of musical language.'[4] He also explained the choice of title: it was 'a serious, non-ironic work, a type of secular Requiem, an expression about death in the form of memorial tablets, epitaphs, and funeral dirges.'[5] That it differed so much from other requiems was due to the new, unusual perspective Brecht and Weill had adopted: 'The content of *Das Berliner Requiem* unquestionably corresponds to the sentiments and perceptions of the broadest level of the population. We attempted to express what the urban man of our era has to say about the phenomenon of death.'[6]

Weill was well acquainted with the radio – then still a relatively new phenomenon. Alongside the *Berliner Requiem* he wrote several other pieces for radio performances while from 1925-9 he was a contributor to the weekly radio guide *Der deutsche Rundfunk*, writing regular previews and reviews of programmes as well as occasionally longer essays. In several of these – including 'A Note Concerning *Das Berliner Requiem*' – he reflects on the different requirements that music has to take into account in order to be successful in the new medium. Foremost among the composer's considerations is the broader nature of the listenership that is not restricted to what Weill calls the 'cultured and affluent classes'; instead

> the radio audience is composed of all classes of people. Consequently, it is impossible to apply the assumptions of the concert hall to radio music. ... For the first time radio poses for the serious musician of the present the task of creating works which can be taken up by as large a circle of listeners as possible. The content and form of these radio compositions must also be capable of interesting a large number of people of all classes; and the means of musical expression must not cause any difficulty for the untrained listener.[7]

Weill also reflects on how the composer can achieve this broader appeal; experience has taught him that too much complexity of texture is to be avoided. Among the aspects pivotal for a composer are

> knowledge of the acoustical restrictions of the broadcasting studio, the orchestral and instrumental capabilities of microphones, the distribution of vocal registers and harmonic limitations that are fixed for a radio composition. Several years of observations when listening to radio music and some of my own efforts have convinced me that this medium is not so much dependent on a particularly crafty technique of instrumentation as on the clarity and transparency of phrasing and texture.[8]

These insights clearly left their mark on the *Berliner Requiem*. Another concept that had a great influence on this work is *Gebrauchsmusik* – a term that is difficult to translate. Both 'functional music' and 'utility music' only capture certain aspects of its meaning. It stands for an attempt by composers in Weimar Germany (including Weill, Eisler and Hindemith) to develop a musical style that would overcome the division between art music and all other musics which were regarded as serving extra-musical functions (such as dancing, marching or working), being listened to as a backdrop to some other activity rather than in focused contemplation. In his article 'Opera – Where to?' (published in October 1929) Weill defined *Gebrauchsmusik* as

> music that is capable of satisfying the musical needs of broader levels of the population without giving up artistic substance. ... we have not contented ourselves with simplifying our means of expression a little. We have, in fact, put aside aesthetic appraisal. In our music we want to allow men of our time to speak, and they ought to speak to many. The first question for us: is what we do useful to the general public? It is only a secondary question if what we create is art, for that is determined only by the quality of our work.[9]

Yet although Weill here calls the artistic nature of this music secondary he insists on the presence of intellectual content: 'under no circumstances should the impression be created that we want to renounce the intellectual bearing of the serious musician in order to compete fully with the producers of lighter market wares.'[10] In fact, Weill proceeds to describe those 'lighter market wares' as 'Verbrauchsmusik' (music to be 'used up') while for him real *Gebrauchsmusik* is only that which successfully negotiates the gap between art music and 'Verbrauchsmusik'. Stephen Hinton summarizes the effect of *Gebrauchsmusik* according to Weill as 'provocative' rather than 'enticing' (hence not just entertaining but conveying a message that will initiate intellectual thought processes in the listener), and Weill proceeds to explain that

> the effect of this music is not catchy, but instead rousing; that the intellectual bearing of this music is thoroughly serious, bitter accusing, and, in the most pleasant cases still ironic; that neither the poetry of this music nor the form of the music itself would be conceivable without the vast background of an ethical or social nature on which it is based.[11]

Musically *Gebrauchsmusik* was based on an avoidance of complexity (such as polyphonic textures or elaborate formal structures), the inclusion of elements of popular music styles such as jazz or dances and often (specifically in the case of Hindemith) a compositional style that made the pieces accessible to non-professional performers.

There is no definitive version of the *Berliner Requiem*; the composer revised the score several times over a number of years without determining a conclusive final version.[12] In the 'Note' he announced a version including 'Vom Tod im Wald' (About Death in the Forest) as opening movement, followed by 'Können einem toten Mann nicht helfen' (Can't help a Dead Man). But at the performance five days later 'Vom Tod im Wald' had been removed (eventually it ended up as a self-standing cantata) while an additional march, 'Zu Potsdam unter den Eichen' (In Potsdam under the Oak Trees), had been added as a new closing number. 'Können einem toten Mann nicht helfen' later became part of *Rise and Fall of the City of Mahagonny* while the composer re-arranged 'Zu Potsdam unter den Eichen' und published it separately. This leaves the five movements that David Drew arranged and revised for publication with Universal Edition in 1967 (with the opening 'Großer Dankchoral' (Grand Hymn of Thanksgiving) being repeated at the end to make it six); in this version the piece is about twenty minutes long (and designated a 'small cantata').

Das Berliner Requiem is scored for modest forces: three male soloists, a male choir (although the choruses can be performed by the soloists as well) and an ensemble consisting of two clarinets, two saxophones, two bassoons, two horns, two trumpets, two trombones, timpani, a guitar, a banjo, cymbals, a small side drum and an organ or a harmonium – yet no strings. Guitar and banjo as the only stringed instruments feature in just one movement each, providing a quasi-basso continuo chordal accompaniment of the vocal parts.

Großer Dankchoral (Great Hymn of Thanksgiving)

The *Berliner Requiem*'s opening chorus is a parody of the Lutheran hymn 'Lobe den Herren, den mächtigen König der Ehren' (Praise to the Lord, the Almighty, the King of Creation). A mainstay of Lutheran congregational singing to this day, the five verses of this hymn (written by Joachim Neander and published in 1680) are sung in a relatively quick tempo in 9/4 time on a diatonic melody which is possibly based on a folk tune. Upward leaps of a fifth (after the first two notes and again after the second phrase) underscore the text's positive and optimistic attitude; it is a song of praise for the Lord, giving thanks for the way in which his love and his blessing guard the singer, granting health and leading her/him through a range of perils and threats.

Bertolt Brecht was, of course, an atheist; critique of religion – particularly in its institutionalized form – was a regular and important part of his work as a poet and playwright (for example in *Leben des Galilei / Life of Galileo*). At the same time he was very familiar with the bible as well as Lutheran traditions (a knowledge instilled into him by his mother and his maternal grandmother, both Lutherans – his father was a Catholic), and both his epic style and his extraordinary power as a wordsmith have repeatedly been related to the language of Luther's German bible. Thomas O. Brandt points out that in 1928 Brecht responded to a journal's invitation to reflect on which book had influenced him the most with a single line: 'You will find it laughable: the bible'.[13] Brandt adds that Brecht studied the bible's language and content all his life. He repeatedly parodied hymns by inventing new texts that could be sung on existing tunes; his six *Hitler Choräle* (Hitler Hymns) from 1933, for example, are based on well-known hymns such as 'Befiehl du deine Wege' (Commit thy Way unto the Lord), 'Ein feste Burg ist unser Gott' (A Mighty Fortress is our God) or again 'Lobe den Herren' while the texts attack the new rulers' policies and uncover their hypocrisies.[14]

In the 'Großer Dankchoral' Weill changed the original hymn's tune considerably; in fact, very few sections (such as the beginning of the last phrase) remind the listener of the original melodic structure (Brecht's text is two lines shorter than Neander's, hence Weill omits the repeat of the first section of the melody). Melodic steps go downward more often than upward, the optimistic larger upward leaps are gone and virtually all larger intervals within phrases leap down. Together with the slower tempo (sostenuto) and the dominance of low voices the music immediately gives the impression of funereal music, thus mocking the 'thanksgiving' mentioned in the title straight away. This is also supported by the harmonic language: the harmonies provided by the three-part choir and the accompanying instruments rarely consist of pure major or minor chords; and wherever major or minor chords appear they are not part of standard harmonic chord progressions. Instead, the majority of chords either consist of incomplete triads (often lacking a third; for example, the chorale ends on the pitches of E and B), diminished ones or triads in which one pitch is raised or lowered (often consisting of a third and a fourth over a root, or a fifth and a sixth over a root). This practice (that applies to all movements) results in a mix of archaic-sounding and dissonant chords that can, however, often be perceived as 'almost correct' with just a single 'wrong' note – possibly a musical realization of Brecht's alienation effect ('Verfremdung') in which the audience's expectations are disappointed in order to make them aware of those expectations and consider possible alternatives.

The four stanzas of Brecht's text completely invert the mood of Neander's original. God is not mentioned at all – instead the bad memory of heaven is praised, alongside night and darkness, grass and animals, and cold and ruin. The listener is told that her/his day (= life) is over, that our lives are akin to those of plants and animals, and that we can die easily since no one recalls us anymore. The most chilling line of this chorale – and perhaps of the entire *Berliner Requiem* – is the penultimate one: 'Es kommt nicht auf euch an' (You do not matter). That heaven has forgotten both our face and our name – that is, our individuality – is also an important thought that will be referred to again in subsequent movements.

Ballade 'Vom ertrunkenen Mädchen' (Ballad 'Of the Drowned Girl')

The four stanzas of this ballad describe the gradual decomposition of a drowned girl's body as it drifts along a stream and later a river. We do not learn what caused her drowning, only what happens to her body afterwards: plants and fish attach themselves to her, contributing to her eventual complete decomposition. There are moments that appear almost like consolation: the sky seems to appease the corpse, and morning and evening are still occurring for her. But all of this is eclipsed by the end of the process: the vanishing of her face, her hands and finally her hair lead to her being gradually forgotten even by God. It is interesting that the loss of the face again occupies a central position here; obviously Brecht regards the loss of our individuality that is symbolized by our faces as a central component of what we fear in death.

'The Drowned Girl' may remind the reader of Ophelia, but Brecht's poem (written in 1920) was originally dedicated to the memory of Rosa Luxemburg, a communist leader involved in the Spartacist uprising in post-war Berlin who – together with Karl Liebknecht – was murdered by paramilitary 'Freikorps' soldiers on 15 January 1919. Her body was thrown into Berlin's Landwehr Canal and only discovered there in a highly decomposed state more than four months later on 1 June. That Brecht and Weill included this poem in the *Berliner Requiem* indicates that their work was meant to commemorate not just the end of the war but also the victims of the Sparticist revolt. While Luxemburg is not actually named in the text, Roland Sanders points out that Brecht planned to use another poem in the *Berliner Requiem* that would have named her, yet had to abstain from that as it might have made the performance impossible.

> Brecht even prepared an alternative text ... dealing specifically with 'Rote Rosa' ('Red Rosa' Luxemburg). This unexpected orientation of the material made the radio authorities uncomfortable, and performance of the piece was postponed several times before it was finally broadcast, without the new 'Red Rosa' text, on May 22, 1929.[15]

The reference to Luxemburg would have made the ideological position of author and composer very clear and also provided a clear content-related trajectory, with movements two and three engaging with the spartacist uprising and movements four and five with the soldiers who fell victim to the war, while the framing hymn adopts the most general stand, not being relatable to any specific incident or period. However, this change – despite going against the composer's intention – allows for a different reading of the overall work. Without the naming of the communist leader the texts of both the second and the third movement can refer to any female victim of violence or war – the text here only mentions her drowning yet not what caused her to end up in the water (Luxemburg was actually shot before being dumped in the canal, so this detail does not fit the historical evidence anyway). We know that soldiers are not the only victims of war – throughout history civilians have often suffered just as much (if not more) during and after wars, and without the Luxemburg reference the unknown woman gradually decomposing in the water could be regarded as any one of them.

Musically this movement is set in a very sparse way – the homophonic lines of the three-part chorus (which significantly aid the comprehensibility of the text) are accompanied only by strummed chords of the guitar. This time many of those chords are 'pure' major or minor triads, yet most of the time they occur in inverted forms – avoiding the root in bass position and therefore giving a subtle impression of never fully settling anywhere until the end. This is reinforced by the movement having no tonal centre, commencing in E minor and finishing in D minor. On the other hand, the setting of the vocal lines indicates a simple and clear formal structure, with the four verses of the poem converted into two musical stanzas in a-b-a-b form.

In its simplified musical setting this movement is perhaps the best example of Weill's dedicated 'radio style' which takes into account the technical and acoustic limitations of radio transmissions at the time (even in the other, more heavily scored movements he often uses the full instrumental forces only in transitional passages between the vocal lines, thus making the text more comprehensible). At the same time the formal clarity of the musical setting is subtly undermined by the harmonic language, thus making this a good example of accessible yet still aesthetically challenging *Gebrauchsmusik*. That this reflection on a woman's decomposing body is sung by a male chorus provides an element of irony. While the dead woman remains without a voice, those singing may well represent the soldiers who killed her (particularly in the light of the relationship between the singing men and the dead, equally voiceless woman in the subsequent movement). When Weill called the composition a 'serious, non-ironic work' in his 'Note on the *Berliner Requiem*' this may have been an ironic remark in itself; after all, in his definition of *Gebrauchsmusik* quoted above he described the genre as 'in the most pleasant cases still ironic'.

Marterl (Epitaph)

The third movement is based on a very brief text. A 'Marterl' indicates rhymed memorial tablets or plaques that can be found in places where someone died, usually in nature. It is a dialectal word used in Bavaria and certain regions of Austria. This one reminds the reader of Johanna Beck who lost her virginity (it is unclear whether due to rape or prostitution), and who committed suicide in reaction to what men had done to her. Maybe she was on the way to becoming another Mother Courage yet didn't have the required courage or sangfroid for this path. The text concludes with a highly ironic 'Ruhe sanft' (rest in peace). Again war does not feature directly in this text, but the treatment of women described here has been an inevitable aspect of war since human beings started fighting each other in groups. Brecht and Weill continue to pursue a focus on those who do not actually fight in wars, yet are their victims just as much as the soldiers. Weill substituted this text for the originally intended second poem about Rosa Luxemburg which would have named her yet was rejected by the Frankfurt broadcasting authorities.

The composer sets this brief poem as a slow waltz, almost a valse triste, that unfolds in three sixteen-bar sections before concluding with a ten-bar coda. For the first time instruments play a major role here – the first section is entirely instrumental. While the waltz rhythm is mainly provided by the brass instruments, the vocal part is this time accompanied by banjo chords. On top of this the two saxophones and the clarinet alternate in providing a typical Weillian half-ironic, bittersweet melody that could easily feature in *Rise and Fall of the City of Mahagonny* or *The Threepenny Opera*: long note values commencing at the beginning of a bar are regularly introduced by a semiquaver upbeat, giving the impression of a limping movement, or perhaps a push that moves a rather sluggish melodic movement forward. The tenor's vocal line is slightly more lively and through-composed, moving mainly downwards in steps (alongside a few upward leaps to gain space for new gradual downward movement). In operas or songs the tenor voice normally represents the youthful, heroic and ardent lover, so its use in this context is rather ironic, but Weill improves on this alienating effect with the final 'Ruhe sanft' which is presented in pianissimo by the three-part male choir. Their calls are the only elements in this movement that display an apparent positive attitude as they move two steps upward, perhaps also hinting at the girl's move up to paradise (the movement finishes in D major, having been centred on F minor up to that point). However, the seriousness of their concern is highly questionable for as male singers they represent the group that bears ultimate responsibility for Johanna Beck's death.

Gesänge von dem unbekannten Soldaten unter dem Triumphbogen (Reports Concerning the Unknown Soldier under the Triumphal Arch)

These two movements (which have to be discussed together as they develop a continuous narrative) form the centrepiece of the *Berliner Requiem*. Their texts are much longer (together they total 398 words while all the other movements — including the concluding repeat of the opening chorale — together come only to 349 words); they also cover about 60 per cent of the duration of the overall work.

Based on the structure of the texts, the musical realization of the two reports could follow the model of a Bach passion or cantata, with the first one set as a recitative in which activities are reported (with a few 'turba' moments provided by the male choir representing the soldiers), the second one then resembling an aria offering reflections on what happened and what its consequences are – or ought to be. However, Weill sets the two texts in pretty much the opposite way, starting the fourth movement with an unusal combination of march and arioso with choral elements and continuing in the fifth movement with a recitative (even calling it 'Rezitativ' in the score). The first report is accompanied by all brass, wind and percussion instruments, providing the strongest instrumental power of all movements. They introduce a highly repetitive, dotted one-bar march theme that refers back to the previous 'Ruhe sanft' idea (its first three notes take up the baritone line of that motif), thus linking the march to the epitaph and satirizing it straight away, confirming the identity of those concluding male singers as soldiers. Here Weill lets the music provide additional information that the text itself does not reveal. Variations of this march theme dominate the entire movement. The choir starts with imitative entries – the only time in the entire work that they do not sing their text simultaneously, which would normally be part of the *Gebrauchsmusik* concept (as it is easier to perform and aids comprehensibility). However, here the polyphonic texture indicates the coming together of men from different directions to fight the war – or, as they put it themselves, to kill the unknown soldier which is what for Brecht and Weill war is all about at the end of the day. The unknown soldier is cornered and killed after four years of war (a clear reference to World War I) by 'us', everybody who fought, and in addition even his mother who is cursed for not protesting when he was enlisted. The killers then smash the dead soldier's face so that he was 'keines Menschen Sohn mehr' (could no longer be anyone's son). 'des Menschen Sohn' (son of man) is an attribute often attached to Jesus in the New Testament, so after an 'Amen' confirming the cursing of the mother this is the second biblical reference and might indicate that man would even kill Jesus in war – or that each soldier is worth as much as Jesus in the eyes of Brecht and Weill. In any case, yet again a face is destroyed, and with it identity and individuality vanish. Finally we learn that the main function of burying the unknown soldier under the triumphal arch is to prevent him from rising again on judgement day and – despite now being unrecognisable – accuse his killers of their deed.

While much of the first report spoke self-referentially in the first person plural, the second report addresses the audience directly in second person plural, now reflecting on the murder's relevance for all listeners. It comments on what was just said before: yes, the soldier was killed, and yes, until the murderers destroyed his face he was just like we all are, but their fear of him returning on judgement day is misplaced since he won't come back, and there won't be a judgement day. The dead stay dead, and nothing can change what happened, but now the speaker pleads with the murderers – us, the audience – not to embark on arguments and to avoid triumphant yelling since both remind the speaker of the victim (which he would otherwise have forgotten already), and also of the identity of the murderers who are still not killed themselves. The movement ends with the question: 'And yet, why haven't you been [killed like him]?' This chilling line is sung completely unaccompanied.

Musically the movement is indeed set as a recitative, sung by the solo baritone – in the first half as a 'recitativo secco' only accompanied by organ or harmonium, in the second half as a 'recitativo accompagnato', that is a melody accompanied by a number of instruments, yet still in the semi-declamatory style of the recitative (rather than the more lyrical style of an aria). Both the bass line in the organ/harmonium part and the bassoon that acts as bass instrument in the accompagnato section repeatedly proceed in a chromatically descending line, a traditional device of funereal music known since Baroque times. The movement's second half is clearly centred on C minor, yet the final instrumental conclusion ends on just two notes: C and B flat above it, finishing on the dissonant interval of a seventh and refusing a release of tension through a consonant tonic chord as would be required in tonal music. There is no happy end here.

The Concept of Necropolitics

How do Brecht and Weill engage with death in the *Berliner Requiem*? Intercession for the deceased and concern about the afterlife are clearly not relevant to them, nor is consolation for those who lost·a loved one. They seem to look not so much at specific, individual deaths but rather at death related to war in general, in some of the many different forms it can take: that of an unknown, anonymous soldier, of an unknown girl whose corpse drifts down a river, or another girl who has a name yet is still unknown to us. What we learn about death is that it destroys our faces, our identity and individuality, that directly or indirectly war makes murderers of us all while the framing thanksgiving hymn reminds us that no individual matters – probably not just in war, but also in the world as it is structured today in general. Of course, the purpose of all this is not to leave us deeply depressed, but rather to get us thinking and maybe even doing something about it ('the effect of this music is not catchy, but instead rousing' as Weill put it in his definition of *Gebrauchsmusik* quoted above – although it arguably is catchy as well on occasion). The target could be to help preventing death of this kind from ever happening again.

But we all have to die, so what kind of death is it that can be prevented here? It is a death that is not so much a biological necessity but a man-made calamity, a dying not of individuals but of large numbers of people at once, and before the time at which they would have been expected to die of natural causes (a statement that can only be made statistically in relation to large numbers of people and not about an individual). An engagement with this kind of death can be observed in many compositions engaging with death in the twentieth and twenty-first centuries, and it indicates a radical shift in the concept of death that artists engage with. This shift can be better understood by reference to a term developed by postcolonial theory, though Herbert Marcuse already theorized this issue sixty years ago, while some ideas by Elias Canetti can also be taken into account.

The concept of *necropolitics*, introduced by the Cameroonian social and political scientist Achille Mbembe in an article in 2003, offers an interesting theoretical approach to an assessment of the *Berliner Requiem*'s socio-political function. As Mbembe states right at the beginning, he regards the power to take decisions about life and death as the most fundamental element of sovereign states.

> This essay assumes that the ultimate expression of sovereignty resides, to a large degree, in the power and the capacity to dictate who may live and who must die. Hence, to kill or to allow to live constitute the limits of sovereignty, its fundamental attributes. To exercise sovereignty is to exercise control over mortality and to define life as the deployment and manifestation of power.[16]

This means, however, that those who exercise sovereign rights, who act on behalf of a nation or polity – be they monarchs, dictators, democratically elected politicians, members of the judiciary or other representatives at administrative levels below the very top – demonstrate their exercising of those rights through condemning certain people to death while letting others live. Mbembe is interested in the mechanics of these death-related policies (or, as he calls them, 'necropolitics').

> But under what practical conditions is the right to kill, to allow to live, or to expose to death exercised? Who is the subject of this right? What does the implementation of such a right tell us about the person who is thus put to death and about the relation of enmity that sets that person against his or her murderer?[17]

As a representative of postcolonial studies, Mbembe is particularly interested in the victims of this process, and – like Brecht and Weill – in how certain groups are particularly prone to become the object of necropolitical acts.

> My concern is those figures of sovereignty whose central project is not the struggle for autonomy but *the generalized instrumentalization of human existence and the material destruction of human bodies and populations*.[18]

Much of Mbembe's thinking is developed on the basis of Michel Foucault's concept of biopower and George Bataille's interpretation of death and sovereignty. According to Bataille, sovereignty can be defined as the ability to transgress all limits that otherwise exist in society, including that of death. Mbembe quotes Bataille as saying that the sovereign 'is he who is, as if death were not ...'.[19] This means that by taking the decision to end someone's life, the sovereign (as an individual, a class or a colonizing polity) not only endorses his own power but simultaneously affirms that he himself is not subject to these decisions.

Among the examples of necropolitical behaviour discussed by Mbembe are slavery, colonialism and apartheid. Race in particular is highlighted as a central concept utilized by those in power to validate their necropolitical decisions: 'the function of racism is to regulate the distribution of death and to make possible the murderous functions of the state.'[20] Colonies and supposedly inferior races are being held in a permanent state of exception in which normal European juridical norms do not apply: 'the sovereign right to kill is not subject to any rule in the colonies. In the colonies, the sovereign might kill at any time or in any manner. Colonial warfare is not subject to legal and institutional rules.'[21] Those colonial times are not over yet; as its current most prominent example Mbembe names the Israeli occupation of Palestinian territories which permanently demonstrate the fundamental tenet of necropolitical power: 'sovereignty means the capacity to define who matters and who does not, who is *disposable* and who is not.'[22]

Among the thinkers mentioned by Mbembe are Hegel, Marx, Bataille, Foucault and Fanon. However, two intellectuals whose thoughts could support the concept of necropolitics very well are missing here: Elias Canetti and Herbert Marcuse. In his study *Crowds and Power*[23] Canetti discussed the behaviour of human beings as members of crowds and the way in which power manifests itself in those situations. As part of this, he contemplates the notion of surviving which – according to Canetti – represents an experience of power: we are more powerful than those we have survived. The dream of eternal life does not just stand for the wish to simply live longer, but more importantly for the wish to outlive others.[24] The best way to achieve this is to become a ruler, a holder of power. For Canetti the undisputed ability to take lives at any time and in whichever quantity is what makes power absolute: 'for the autocrat's only true subject is the man who will let himself be killed by him.'[25] At the same time the ruler is the only one whose life is exempt from being taken by anybody else as there is no higher power. However, regular executions are necessary in order to constantly remind people of the ruler's prerogative, so they are organized even if their victims are not really guilty of anything – their death increases the ruler's power in an archaic-direct way (yet again he has survived someone else), but also in an indirect one (everybody else now has a renewed respect for his power).[26] In a dictatorship, the ruler is often paranoid and decides when and whom to kill in a totally arbitrary way as he regards this as the only way to keep control over the people: 'his best, one might say his most perfect subjects are those that died for him.'[27]

It is obvious that Canetti's understanding of the role of death in the relationship between rulers and ruled is very close to Mbembe's concept of necropolitics. Both regard the right to kill as the central attribute of power/sovereignty, and both stress the arbitrary nature in which this right is often enacted – mainly in order to confirm existing power structures. But the modern human being regarded death for a long time as an individual biological inevitability. How did the switch to it being a result of power structures come about? A text by Herbert Marcuse that anticipates many of Mbembe's ideas can help in understanding this change.

In his essay 'The Ideology of Death'[28] (first published in 1959) Marcuse juxtaposed the two 'ideologies' of death: on the one hand there is death as individual fate against which there is no resistance; hence the best way forward is to accept it. On the other hand there is death as the result of the interference of others, namely those in power who create circumstances in which large numbers of people die 'before their time', i.e. before there was a biological necessity to do so. Marcuse places much of the responsibility for this second ideology at Christianity's door: it started its existence as a religion of the lower classes, offering them the hope of a better afterlife which would compensate for injustice and suffering in this life. On this basis death should no longer be feared but rather welcomed. However, at some stage the ruling classes adopted Christianity as their official religion, not least because they sensed its usefulness with regard to the stabilization of existing power structures: 'selling' death to the lower classes as a biological inevitability when it was actually the result of political decisions (such as those leading to war, famine or genocides) made it easier to convince people to die for a 'good cause' such as one's nation, religion or culture – this kind of death could now be propagated as a glorious and desirable act that would be compensated in the afterlife. As long as people accepted death as their individual, purely biological fate they automatically also accepted the existing power structures. If instead they were to regard death as an 'institution', caused by those in power, death could (and should) be fought as part of the class war that the members of the Frankfurt School (of which Marcuse was a prominent representative) were invested in. Fighting death as an institution caused by the ruling class means taking the necropolitical power out of the hands of those that caused so many millions of unnecessary (i.e. premature) deaths in the twentieth century alone.

Of course, even after a change of power structures and institutions people would still die – insofar Marcuse's claims may go a bit far. His first ideology of death as individual fate against which there is no resistance is certainly not based on indoctrination alone but simply on the fact that it is true, that we all have to die eventually regardless of societal structures and our respective systems of government. But he is right in claiming that religion's promise of an afterlife facilitated the attempts of societal and political forces to convince people that both dying and killing 'for a good cause' are desirable things, and also that those in power have regularly shortened the lives of many who would otherwise have lived much longer. What is to be resisted is not death as inevitable biological end of life that we all have to face, but rather avoidable premature deaths that occur earlier than biologically necessary and are caused by political or ideological decisions. Fighting against those (ab)uses of power as Marcuse and ultimately also Brecht and Weill see it is certainly a worthwhile cause.

Necropolitics and the *Berliner Requiem*

The *Berliner Requiem* clearly engages with death in a necropolitical way, addressing those who are on the receiving end of the decisions of Canetti's and Mbembe's death-wielding rulers and classes, pointing out that war causes the death of many, that there is no glory or any kind of achievement in dying or indeed causing the deaths of others, and that in war everybody ends up guilty. But there are two levels of guilt here: Brecht and Weill make it very clear that they regard the deaths caused by soldiers in war as murder, and that even a mother who does not object to her son being conscripted comes to share in the responsibility of his death. But ultimately this is caused by the existing power structures, so the guilt of all those people actually undertaking the murders lies less in their deeds but in their decision to let those power structures persist. The framing 'Great Hymn of Thanksgiving' seems to indicate that 'you' – the common people mainly addressed by Brecht and Weill – don't matter even while still alive, and while this is not developed further one can infer from the communist leanings of both that they would like people to start contemplating a change of societal and power structures in order to deprive those people of power who reach bad necropolitical decisions, such as starting wars. This is most likely what Weill referred to when he wrote shortly before the premiere '[t]he content of *Das Berliner Requiem* unquestionably corresponds to the sentiments and perceptions of the broadest level of the population. We attempted to express what the urban man of our era has to say about the phenomenon of death'. However, maybe it would be more correct to say what the urban man (interestingly the rural dweller is left out here, perhaps due to her/his traditionally more conservative leanings) *should have* to say about the phenomenon of death since certainly not all members of the middle and lower classes would have agreed with Weill straight away. The piece therefore has an important educational aspect, one which Weill acknowledged in his definition of *Gebrauchsmusik*. The focus on the urban 'man' – while perhaps understandable, given the time at which Brecht wrote his poems – is also disappointing from the point of view of gender equality; however, that fact that the fate of dead women (at least one of whom a victim of men) is addressed in two movements before the fate of men (in the guise of the unknown soldier) comes into focus may make up for that. That war does not just kill those actually doing the fighting but many others as well is one of the important messages of this piece.

Despite the occasional mentioning of god and heaven Brecht and Weill do not believe in an afterlife other than in the memory of those who knew a deceased. Their ultimate death is a social death, the point at which the living no longer remember the dead. By killing people we deprive them of their faces and their identity; they will be forgotten much earlier than necessary – a crime all the more serious if there is no afterlife that could compensate for it.

The music Kurt Weill composed for the *Berliner Requiem* is a very good example of *Gebrauchsmusik* that combines comprehensibility and lack of complexity to make it accessible to listeners not accustomed to listening to art music (those not belonging to Weill's 'cultured and affluent classes'). At the same time it is original and full of subtle aesthetic details that help creating Brechtian alienation effects and support the work's educational, 'provocative' and 'bitter accusing' purpose. The lack of complexity in terms of musical structure and instrumentation conforms to Weill's ideas with regard to music composed for transmission on radio. That the piece is rarely performed today may have to do with its having effectively been withdrawn and thus remaining virtually unknown until long after Weill's death, yet perhaps even more with its uncompromising, bleak texts that could leave some listeners feeling uncomfortable (while also securing its deep impact if one is prepared to engage with them).

For Brecht and Weill the premature deaths of millions such as those caused by the First World War are pointless, unnecessary and should be prevented from ever occurring again in the future. Of course, we know that exactly the opposite is what happened not long after both had to leave Germany in 1933, but that doesn't make Brecht and Weill's *Berliner Requiem* a less honourable attempt at highlighting this point – and one that is still worth our attention today.

Note
I would like to thank Alexandra Monchick for her advice regarding literature on Weill in the early stages of my research.
Several recordings of the *Berliner Requiem* are available online.

[1] Quoted in Jürgen Schebera, *Kurt Weill: An Illustrated Life*, transl. C. Murphy (New Haven: Yale University Press, 1995), 126.
[2] Roland Sanders, *The Life and Music of Kurt Weill* (New York: Holt, Rinehart and Winston, 1980), 132.
[3] Kurt Weill, 'A Note Concerning *Das Berliner Requiem*', in *Kurt Weill in Europe*, Studies in Musicology No. 14, ed. Kim Kowalke (Ann Arbor: UMI Research Press, 1979), 503-505. Originally published in German as 'Notiz zum Berliner Requiem', in *Der deutsche Rundfunk* 7 (7 May 1929), 613. The German version is published in *Kurt Weill. Ausgewählte Schriften*, ed. David Drew (Frankfurt am Main: Suhrkamp, 1975), 139-141.
[4] Weill, 'A Note', 503.
[5] *Ibid.*, 504.
[6] *Ibid.*
[7] *Ibid.*
[8] *Ibid.*, 503.
[9] 'Opera – Where to?', in *Kurt Weill in Europe*, Studies in Musicology No. 14, ed. Kim Kowalke (Ann Arbor: UMI Research Press, 1979), 506-509: 506. Originally published as 'Die Oper – Wohin?', in *Berliner Tageblatt*, 31 October 1929.
[10] *Ibid.*, 507.
[11] *Ibid.*, 507. Hinton's article contains a detailed discussion of the term 'Gebrauchsmusik' in relation to Weill. See Stephen Hinton, 'Weill: *Neue Sachlichkeit*, Surrealism and *Gebrauchsmusik*', in *A New Orpheus. Essays on Kurt Weill*, ed. Kim Kowalke (New Haven, London: Yale University Press, 1986), 61-82.
[12] For a summary of the version history see David Drew, 'Editor's Preface', in *Kurt Weill: Das Berliner Requiem*, score (Vienna: Universal Edition, 1976), vi-vii.
[13] 'Sie werden lachen: die Bibel.' Thomas O. Brandt, 'Brecht und die Bibel', in *PMLA* 79/1 (March 1964), 171-176: 171. Translation by the author.
[14] Brandt, 'Brecht und die Bibel', 172.
[15] Roland Sanders, *The Life and Music of Kurt Weill* (New York: Holt, Rinehart and Winston, 1980), 132.
[16] Achille Mbembe, 'Necropolitics', transl. Libby Meintjes, in *Public Culture* 15/1 (2003), 11-40: 11-12.
[17] *Ibid.*, 12.
[18] *Ibid.*, 14. Emphasis in the original.
[19] *Ibid.*, 8.
[20] *Ibid.*, 17.
[21] *Ibid.*, 25.
[22] *Ibid.*, 27.
[23] Elias Canetti, *Crowds and Power*, transl. Carol Stewart (London: Gollancz, 1962). First published in German as *Masse und Macht* in 1960.
[24] *Ibid.*, 227-8.
[25] *Ibid.*, 232. The original German sentence reads 'denn wirklich unterworfen ist ihm nur, wer sich von ihm töten läßt', Elias Canetti, *Masse und Macht* (Frankfurt/M.: Fischer, 1992), 255.
[26] *Ibid.*, 233.
[27] *Ibid.*
[28] Herbert Marcuse, 'The Ideology of Death', in *The Meaning of Death*, ed. Hermann Feifel (New York: McGraw Hill, 1959), 64-76.

Das Berliner Requiem - Text

1) Grosser Dankchoral

Lobet die Nacht
und die Finsternis, die Euch umfangen!
Kommet zuhauf!
Schaut in dem Himmel hinauf:
Schon ist der Tag euch vergangen.

Lobet von Herzen
das schlechte Gedächtnis des Himmels!
Und dass er nicht
Weiss Euren Nam' noch Gesicht
Niemand weiss, dass ihr noch da seid.

Lobet das Gras und die Tiere,
Die neben euch leben und sterben!
Sehet wie ihr,
lebet das Gras und das Tier.
Und es muss auch mit euch sterben.

Lobet die Kälte,
Die Finsternis und das Verderben!
Schauet hinan:
Es kommt nicht auf euch an.
Und ihr könnt unbesorgt sterben.

2) Ballade "Vom ertrunkenen Mädchen"

Als sie ertrunken war und hinunterschwamm
Von den Bächen in die größeren Flüsse,
schien der Opal des Himmels sehr wundersam,
als ob er die Leiche begütigen müsse.

Great Hymn of Thanksgiving

Give praise to the night
and darkness that close around you.
Crowd together
and look up at the sky and see that the day has already slipped away from you.

Give praise from the bottom of your heart that heaven has a bad memory,
and no longer knows
either your names or your faces,
and that nobody knows that you are still around.

Praise the grass and the beasts
that live and die beside you.
See how the grass,
and the beasts, too, live
and, like you, must also die.

Give praise for the cold,
the darkness and corruption!
Look up!
You do not matter, and you can die without worrying about a thing.

Ballad "Of the Drowned Girl"

When she drowned and floated down
from the streams to the bigger rivers
the opalescent sky looked astonishing,
as if it had to appease the corpse.

Tang und Algen hielten sich an ihr ein,	Seaweed clung to her
So daß sie langsam viel schwerer ward.	so that she gradually grew heavier.
Kühl die Fische schwammen an ihrem Bein	The cool fishes swam about her legs
Pflanzen und Tiere beschwerten noch ihre letzte Fahrt.	and her last journey was made even heavier by plants and animals.
Und der Himmel ward abends dunkel wie Rauch	And in the evening the sky became dark as smoke
Und hielt nachts mit den Sternen das Licht in der Schwebe.	and at night almost obscured the light of the stars.
Aber früh war er hell, damit es auch für sie noch Morgen und Abend gebe.	But it grew bright early, so that for her, too, there would be a morning and an evening
Als ihr bleicher Leib im Wasser verfaulet war	When her pale body had putrefied in the water
geschah es (sehr langsam), daß Gott sie allmählich vergaß	God very slowly began to forget her:
Erst ihr Gesicht, dann die Hände und zuletzt erst ihr Haar.	First her face, then her hands, and only in the end her hair.
Dann ward sie Aas in Flüssen mit vielen Aas.	Then she was carrion in rivers full of carrion

3) Marterl (Grabinschrift) — Epitaph

Hier ruht die Jungfrau Johanna Beck.	Here rests the virgin Johanna Beck.
Als sie starb, war ihre Unschuld schon vorher weg.	Before she died she had already lost her innocence.
Die Männer haben ihr den Rest gegeben.	The men finished her off,
Drum floh sie aus diesem süssen Leben.	and that is why she run away from this sweet life
Ruhe sanft.	Rest in peace.

4) Erster Gesang von dem unbekannten Soldaten unter dem Triumphbogen

Wir kamen von den Gebirgen und vom Weltmeer,
um ihn zu erschlagen.
Wir fingen ihn mit Stricken, langend
Von Moskau bis zur Stadt Marseille.

Und stellten auf Kanonen, ihn erreichend
An jedem Punkt, wo er hinfliehen konnte,
Wenn er uns sah.

Wir vesammelten uns vier Jahre lang
Legten nieder unsere Arbeit und standen
In den zerfallenden Städten, uns zurufend in vielen Sprachen
Von den Gebirgen bis zum Weltmeer,
Wo er sei.
So erschlugen wir ihn im vierten Jahr.

Dabei waren,
Die er war geboren zu sehn
Um sich stehend zur Zeit seines Todes:
Wir alle.
Und dabei war eine Frau, die ihn geboren hatte
Und die geschwiegen hatte, als wir ihn holten.
Der Schoß sei ihr ausgerissen!
Amen!

Als wir ihn aber erschlagen hatten
Richteten wir ihn zu, daß er sein Gesicht verlor
Durch die Spuren unsrer Fäuste.
So machten wir ihn unkenntlich

First Report Concerning the Unknown Soldier under the Triumphal Arch

We came from the mountains and the oceans
to kill him.
We caught him with snares reaching
from Moscow as far as the city of Marseille

And we set up guns pointing in every direction
to which he could escape
when he saw us.

For four years we came together,
gave up our work and stood around
in the disintegrating towns, calling to each other in many languages
from the mountains and the oceans
where he could be.
Then, in the fourth year we killed him.

Those he was born to see standing about him at the time of his death
were present.
All of us.
And a woman was there, who had given him birth
and had been silent when we took him.
May her womb be ripped out of her!
Amen!

Then, after we had killed him,
we smashed him up so that he had no face left
from the blows of our fists.
In this way we made him unrecognizable

Daß er keines Menschen Sohn mehr sei.	So that he could no longer be anyone's son
Und gruben ihn aus unter dem Erz	And we dug him out from under the ore,
Trugen ihn heim in unsere Stadt und Begruben ihn unter dem Stein, und zwar unter einem Bogen genannt Bogen des Triumphs.	carried him home to our town and buried him under the stone, under an arch called arch of triumph.
Welcher wog tausend Zentner, daß Der unbekannte Soldat Keinesfalls aufstünde am Tag des Gerichts	It weighed a thousand hundredweight, so that there was no way the Unknown Soldier could rise up again on the Day of Judgement
Und unkenntlich wandelte vor Gott Dennoch wieder im Licht Und bezeichnete uns Kenntliche Zur Gerechtigkeit.	and, unrecognizable, walk up to God back in the light again, and point us out as the ones to be brought to justice.

5) Zweiter Gesang von dem unbekannten Soldaten unter dem Triumphbogen

Second Report Concerning the Unknown Soldier under the Triumphal Arch

Alles, was ich euch sagte über Ermordung und Tod des Unbekannten Soldaten Und die Verwüstung seines Gesichts, Auch was ich euch sagte über die Bemühung seiner Mörder Ihn zu hindern am Wiederkommen, Ist wahr, aber: Er kommt nicht wieder.	Everything I told you about the murder and death of the Unknown Soldier, and the mutilation of his face, and also what I told you about the efforts of his murderers to prevent his return, is true, but: he will not come back.
Sein Gesicht war lebending wie das eure, bis es zerschmettert wurde und nicht mehr war. Und es ward Nicht mehr gesehn auf dieser Welt, Weder ganz noch zerschmettert	His face was alive as yours until he was shattered and ceased to exist and was not seen again in this world, either whole or shattered,

Weder heute noch am Ende der Tage,	either today or at the end of time.
Und sein Mund	And his mouth
Wird nicht reden am Jüngsten Gericht:	will not speak at the Last Judgement:
Es wird	there will
Kein Gericht sein.	be no judgement.
Sondern euer Bruder	For your brother
Ist tot und tot	is dead, and dead
Ist der Stein über ihm	is the stone covering him,
Und ich bedaure	and I regret
Jeglichen Hohn, und ziehe zurück meine Klage.	every insult, and withdraw my complaint
Aber ich bitte euch, da ihr ihn	But I beg you,
Nun einmal erschlagen habt,	now that you have killed him.
Still, fangt nicht von neuem an	Quiet, don't start arguing
Zu streiten, da er doch tot ist.	again, now that he is dead after all.
Aber doch bitte ich, da ihr ihn also	I beg you, since you have
Erschlagen habt:	killed him,
Entfernt wenigstens	at least remove
Den Stein über ihm	the stone that covers him,
Denn dieses Triumphgeheul	because all this triumphant yelling
Ist doch nicht nötig und macht	isn't really necessary and
Mir Kummer, denn mich,	just troubles me,
Der ich den Erschlagenen	because every day he reminds me,
Schon vergessen hatte, erinnert er	who had already forgotten him,
Täglich an euch, die ihr	of you who are still alive and
Immer noch nicht erschlagen seid -	not yet have been killed.
Warum denn nicht?	And yet, why haven't you been?

English translation by Derek Yeld, published in the 1992 Harmonia Mundi recording of *Das Berliner Requiem* (HMC 901422), as quoted in Magnar Breivik, 'Brecht and Weill's *Das Berliner Requiem*. A Secular Work in a Sacred Tradition', in *Genre and Ritual. The Cultural Heritage of Medieval Rituals*, special issue of *Transfiguration: Nordic Journal for Christianity and the Arts*, 1/2 (2003), eds Eyolf Østrem, Mette Birkedal Bruun, Nils Holger Petersen and Jens Fleischer (Copenhagen: Museum Tusculanum Press, 2005), 274-88.

Contributors

Alan Baird was born in Scotland and raised in rural Galloway (the closest traffic lights and the nearest cinema were across the sea in Ireland). Having trained at the Universities of Glasgow, London and Cambridge, Alan is a pharmacologist who heads Veterinary Sciences as Professor of Veterinary Physiology & Biochemistry in Ireland's only School of Veterinary Medicine at University College Dublin. He is active in the One Health agenda expanding interdisciplinary collaborations and communications in aspects of health care for humans, animals and the environment. He has published over 100 research papers and has enjoyed the privilege of mentoring many undergraduate and postgraduate students.

Joseph Brady is a geographer, whose main interests lie in the study of urban areas. He has made a particular study of Dublin and is both editor (and author) of a book series entitled the *Making of Dublin City*. The seven volumes explore the city both chronologically and thematically and an eighth volume, focusing on the developmental 'lens' of key builders, will soon appear. He was, for many years, editor of *Irish Geography*, President of the Geographical Society of Ireland and is a collector of maps, documents and ephemera relating to Dublin. The paper in this book reflects his interest in maps, which are not just an aid to travel but are often fascinating political, social and historical documents.

Dan Farrelly completed his doctorate in Strasbourg in 1970, then worked as a Lecturer in German at University College Dublin before becoming Director of the UCD Drama Studies Centre in 1995. He is currently General Editor and a Director of Carysfort Press. His publications include *Goethe and Inner Harmony* (1973); *Schöne Seele Studies: Essays on Goethe* (1978); *Goethe in East Germany, 1949-1989: Towards A History of Goethe Reception in the GDR* (1998); *Between Myth and Reality: Goethe, Anna Amalia, Charlotte von Stein* (2010); a translation of David Asher's book on *New Material by Schopenhauer and about Schopenhauer* (2015); his German translation of *Between Myth and Reality* is to be published in 2017 with LiteraturWissenschaft.de. He has translated a trilogy of theological works by the Jesuit Roger Lenaers, appearing currently with Carysfort Press. He has also translated plays by Goethe, Büchner, and Wedekind as well as 11 books of the German philosopher, Josef Pieper, for St. Augustine's Press, South Bend.

Andreas Hess teaches sociology at University College Dublin. He is the author of *The Political Theory of Judith N. Shklar. Exile from Exile* (New York: Palgrave, 2014) and (with Tom Garvin) the editor of Gustave de Beaumont's *Ireland* (Cambridge, MA: Belknap Press of Harvard University Press, 2006). He is currently working on a book on *Tocqueville, Beaumont and the Birth Pangs of Modern Democracy* for Palgrave's Pivot Series (to be published in the autumn of 2017).

Michael Laffan studied in University College Dublin, Trinity Hall Cambridge, and the Institute for European History in Mainz. He lectured in the University of East Anglia in Norwich, and then, for over three decades, in UCD. He served as head of the School of History, he was president of the Irish Historical Society between 2010 and 2012, and he is now an emeritus professor. His writings include *The Partition of Ireland* (1983), *The Resurrection of Ireland: the Sinn Féin Party, 1916-23* (1999), and *Judging W.T. Cosgrave* (2014). He has also edited *The Burden of German History, 1919-1945* (1988). He has lectured widely throughout Ireland and across the globe.

Sheryl Lynch earned her IRC-funded PhD in ethnomusicology from University College Dublin in 2016. Her research interests include music and migration, life cycle rituals, and music and intersectionality. Sheryl has published work in *Public and Political Discourses of Migration* (2016) and *The Canadian Graduate Journal for Social Justice* (2016). She has presented her research at conferences held by the Institute for Gender, Race, Sexuality and Social Justice (UBC, Vancouver), and the International Association for the Study of Popular Music, UK. During her doctoral studies, she served as Education Officer for the International Council for Traditional Music, Ireland, in addition to lecturing at St Patrick's College, Drumcondra. Sheryl has co-edited *The Musicology Review* and edited ICTM's online bulletin, *Spéis*. Most recently, her paper on women's music in Cameroon formed part of a panel on refugee narratives at the annual meeting of the American Anthropological Association in Minneapolis. She currently lectures in minority musics and popular music at the University of Nottingham.

Wolfgang Marx lectures in Musicology at University College Dublin's School of Music, as well as being a member of the UCD Humanities Institute. He also chairs the research strand 'Death, Burial and the Afterlife' at the UCD College of Arts & Humanities. His research interests include the representation of death in music (with a special focus on requiem compositions), the music of György Ligeti and the theory of musical genres. Among his recent publications are *Rethinking Hanslick. Music, Formalism, and Expression* (co-edited with Nicole Grimes and Siobhán Donovan, 2013) and *Death, Burial and the Afterlife. Dublin Death Studies 1* (co-edited with Philip Cottrell, 2014).

Corinna Ricasoli is an Italian art historian. The recipient of a postgraduate scholarship from the Irish Research Council for the Humanities and Social Sciences, she attained her PhD from the School of Art History & Cultural Policy, University College Dublin, Ireland. Her thesis *'Non Omnis Moriar': Artists' Funerary Monuments in Baroque Rome*, examines the artist's concern with identity, mortality, and a posthumous reputation in Rome between the late sixteenth and early eighteenth centuries. She has worked at the Musée du Louvre, Paris, and has frequently been invited to guest lecture at several European institutions, including UCD, National Gallery of Ireland, and Università degli Studi di Roma Tor Vergata. She holds research associateships at the UCD Humanities Institute and at the Vatican Apostolic Library (Cabinet of Prints & Drawings), where she is drawing up a complete catalogue of Giovanni Battista Piranesi's prints for publication. She is currently Consultant Curator of Fine Arts, Museum of the Bible, Washington DC.

Illustrations

Fig. 1.1) Charles Stewart Parnell's funeral procession crossing O'Connell Bridge in Dublin. Finerty, J.F. (1898) *Ireland in Pictures: A Grand Collection of Over 400 Magnificent Photographs of the Beauties of the Green Isle, with Historical and Descriptive Sketches.* New York: J.S. Hyland and Co., 90.

Fig. 1.2) A volley of shots is fired at the funeral of Thomas Ashe. Courtesy of the National Library of Ireland.

Fig. 1.3) Terence MacSwiney's funeral procession in London. Courtesy of UCD Archives.

Fig. 1.4) Funeral procession of Michael Collins, Dublin, O'Connell Street. Courtesy of the National Library of Ireland.

Fig. 2.1) Opening dance troupe at Mankon cry-die, July 2012 (Author's photograph).

Fig. 2.2) Soloist at cry-die, July 2012 (Author's photograph).

Fig. 2.3) Photograph of deceased held up by granddaughter at Clondalkin cry-die (Author's photograph, 21st June 2013).

Fig. 3.1) Pietro da Cortona, façade of the Church of Santi Luca e Martina al Foro, c. 1669.

Fig. 3.2) View of the crypt or *Confessio*.

Fig. 3.3) View of the crypt or *Confessio*.

Fig. 3.4) View of the crypt or *Confessio*.

Fig. 3.5) View from behind of the bronze altar in the *Confessio*, designed by Pietro da Cortona, marking the burial site of St Martina and the other martyrs.

Fig. 3.6) Front view of the bronze altar in the *Confessio*, designed by Pietro da Cortona, marking the burial site of St Martina and the other martyrs.

Fig. 3.7) View of the Chapel of St Lazarus.

Fig. 3.8) View of the dome and lantern.

Fig. 3.9) Domenico Martinelli, *Plan of the upper and lower Church of Santi Luca e Martina al Foro, Rome,* c. 1678 – 1690. Pencil, brown ink, pen, wash, 536 x 416 mm. Milan, Civico Gabinetto dei Disegni, Castello Sforzesco, inv. SM_1,3. Copyright Comune di Milano – all rights reserved.

Illustrations

Fig. 3.10) Tomb of Pietro da Cortona, 1669.

Fig. 3.11) View of the main nave of the church and of Pietro da Cortona's tomb.

Fig. 3.12) Cenotaph of Pietro da Cortona in the *Confessio*.

Fig. 3.13) Cenotaph of Pietro da Cortona in the *Confessio* (details of Bernardo Fioriti's bust of Pietro da Cortona, c. 1677).

Fig. 6.1) The pet cemetery in the grounds of Powerscourt House, Co.Wicklow, Ireland. Courtesy of Powerscourt Estates.

Fig. 6.2) Example of tombstone over pet grave in the pet cemetery in the grounds of Powerscourt House. Courtesy of Powerscourt Estates.

Fig. 7.1) Example of 'War Service badge' designed to show that the bearer was involved in essential duties.

Fig. 7.2) The charge of the light cavalry at Balaclava. *Illustrated London News*, 23 December 1854, 676-8.

Fig. 7.3) Cover of the Liberty Map of the Western Front.

Fig. 7.4) Covers of maps in a Daily Express set.

Fig. 7.5) Detail from the cover of the Hammond *War Map Kit*.

Fig. 7.6) The customizing for the *Allied Liberty map of the World at War*.

Fig. 7.7) Two Esso maps, one an 'invasion edition'.

Fig. 7.8) Information panel from Esso map.

Fig. 7.9) Detail from the International Radio News map, showing ranges.

Fig. 7.10) Two versions of the Rand McNally map.

Fig. 7.11) Staleys and the map of Naval and Military Power.

Fig. 7.12) The Erno mini-atlas.

Fig. 7.13) Detail from Esso transportation map.

Fig. 7.14) Gettier Montayne letter to potential customers.

Fig. 7.15) Detail from Dated War Map.

Fig. 7.16) Some examples of Dated War Maps.

Fig. 7.17) Wrapper from Daily Express map series.